Graceful. Poised. Accepting. Poetic. Generous. Open to life's mysteries. These are thoughts that circulated through my mind as I read Bruce Reis' marvelous, monstrous, zombie-filled book. Here is an author who can make the death drive seductive. Reis extends a heartfelt welcome to his patients, to other psychoanalysts working in the field and to his readers. His review of the literature is remarkable for its compassion and insight into the thoughts of others. His clinical vignettes beautifully illuminate worlds of *being together*. For anyone who wants to grasp the vibrant realm of intersubjective psychoanalysis this is a wonderful book.

—**Jonathan Lear**, The University of Chicago, USA

A sparkling and erudite journey through the intersubjective dimension of psychoanalytic work. Reis weaves together the literature from two continents, from Freud to de M'Uzan, from Bion to Ogden and Spezzano. As he does so, illustrating his ideas with artful clinical vignettes, he develops a style and conceptual model that is very much his own, one in which the analyst's presence, openness and even psychic surrender to the patient's communications create the conditions for gradual change. A book well worth reading.

—**Lucy LaFarge**, Regional Editor for North America at the IJP; Clinical Professor of Psychiatry, Weill Cornell Medical College, USA

Creative Repetition and Intersubjectivity is an exceptional book in which Bruce Reis succeeds in freshly approaching the subtle paradox that lies at the core of the analytic process. That paradox involves the tension between the effort on the part of the analyst to open himself or herself as fully as possible in a free and undirected way to what is occurring in the session; and at the same time, to bring to bear on those *forms of experiencing* a disciplined use of the mind with which to gauge the manner and timing in which to make one's presence felt. Reis' clinical discussions crackle with the immediacy, the intimacy, and the danger of true analytic engagement. I cannot recommend this book more highly both to those new to analytic practice and those well-seasoned in that work.

—**Thomas H. Ogden, M. D.**, Author, most recently, of *Reclaiming Unlived Life: Experiences in Psychoanalysis* and *Creative Readings: Essays on Seminal Analytic Works*

Dr. Bruce Reis' book takes the reader on a fascinating journey through the unique territory that is created by the engagement between analyst and analysand at deeply unconscious levels. It is here in the depths of the mind that we become acquainted with the unexpected chimeras and 'monsters' of our psyches, like the unexpected sea creatures living at deep ocean steam vents. Dr. Reis is simply masterful in his ability to access and intricately weave together the valuable contributions of both classical and contemporary psychoanalysts, including Freud, Searles, Winnicott, de M'Uzan, Bion and many others. For those analysts interested in the continued relevance of unconscious processes, Dr. Reis' book is an invaluable companion that is simultaneously an excellent read.

—**Lawrence J. Brown**, Author, *Transformational Processes in Clinical Psychoanalysis: Dreaming, Emotions and the Present Moment*

'Duende' wrote John Berger, 'is a quality, a resonance which makes a performance unforgettable . . .' Such is the quality of *El Duende* present in Bruce Reis's unforgettable book. Here Reis captures the complex, creative and unfolding process of the live analytic encounter. In a movement toward the future of psychoanalysis, Reis takes the reader back in time to a pre-enlightenment ethos in which receptivity to emergent experiences in the field of analysis reveals the surfacing of dynamic unconsciousness in action. His book offers a unique and beautifully written addition to cutting edge analytic theories about the non-conscious, non-verbal dimension of our work and much more.

—**Rachel Peltz**, Faculty and Supervising Analyst, Psychoanalytic Institute of Northern California, San Francisco, USA

Creative Repetition and Intersubjectivity

Creative Repetition and Intersubjectivity looks at contemporary Freudian and post-Freudian theory through an intersubjective lens. Bruce Reis offers views on how psychoanalytic conceptions from the last century uniquely manifest in the consulting rooms of this century – how analytic technique has radically evolved through developing Freud's original insights into dreaming and hallucinosis, and how the presentation of today's analysands calls for analyst's use of themselves in unprecedented new ways.

Taking up bedrock analytic concepts such as the death instinct, repetition, trauma and the place of speech and of silence, Reis brings a diversely inspired, twenty-first century analytic sensibility to his reworking of these concepts and illustrates them clinically in a process-oriented approach. Here the unconscious intersubjective relation takes on transformative power, resulting in the analyst's experience of hybridized chimerical monsters, creative seizures, reveries and intuitions that inform clinical realities outside of verbal or conscious discourse – where change occurs in analysis.

Drawing on an unusually broad selection of major international influences, *Creative Repetition and Intersubjectivity* will be of great interest to psychoanalysts and psychoanalytic psychotherapists across the schools of thought.

Bruce Reis, Ph.D., FIPA, is a Fellow and Faculty Member at the Institute for Psychoanalytic Training and Research, New York, an Adjunct Clinical Assistant Professor in the New York University Postdoctoral Program in Psychotherapy and Psychoanalysis and a member of the Boston Change Process Study Group. He is North American book review editor for the *International Journal of Psychoanalysis* and serves on the editorial boards of *The Psychoanalytic Quarterly* and *Psychoanalytic Dialogues*. He is the co-editor (with Robert Grossmark) of *Heterosexual Masculinities* (Routledge, 2009).

Creative Repetition and Intersubjectivity

Contemporary Freudian
Explorations of Trauma, Memory,
and Clinical Process

Bruce Reis

LONDON AND NEW YORK

First published 2020
by Routledge
2 Park Square, Milton Park, Abingdon, Oxon OX14 4RN

and by Routledge
52 Vanderbilt Avenue, New York, NY 10017

Routledge is an imprint of the Taylor & Francis Group, an informa business

© 2020 Bruce Reis

The right of Bruce Reis to be identified as author of this work has been asserted by him in accordance with sections 77 and 78 of the Copyright, Designs and Patents Act 1988.

All rights reserved. No part of this book may be reprinted or reproduced or utilised in any form or by any electronic, mechanical, or other means, now known or hereafter invented, including photocopying and recording, or in any information storage or retrieval system, without permission in writing from the publishers.

Trademark notice: Product or corporate names may be trademarks or registered trademarks, and are used only for identification and explanation without intent to infringe.

British Library Cataloguing-in-Publication Data
A catalogue record for this book is available from the British Library

Library of Congress Cataloging-in-Publication Data
Names: Reis, Bruce, 1960– author.
Title: Creative repetition and intersubjectivity : contemporary Freudian explorations of trauma, memory, and clinical process / Bruce Reis.
Description: Abingdon, Oxon ; New York, NY : Routledge, 2020. | Includes bibliographical references and index.
Identifiers: LCCN 2019017053 (print) | LCCN 2019019051 (ebook) | ISBN 9780429291555 (Master) | ISBN 9780367261184 (hardback : alk. paper) | ISBN 9780367261207 (pbk. : alk. paper)
Subjects: LCSH: Freud, Sigmund, 1856–1939. | Psychoanalysis. | Intersubjectivity. | Psychic trauma. | Memory.
Classification: LCC BF173.F85 (ebook) | LCC BF173.F85 R438 2020 (print) | DDC 150.19/5—dc23
LC record available at HYPERLINK "https://protect-us.mimecast.com/s/ux1WCDkY05i5ZZZEAF5_tIP?domain=lccn.loc.gov" https://lccn.loc.gov/2019017053

ISBN: 978-0-367-26118-4 (hbk)
ISBN: 978-0-367-26120-7 (pbk)
ISBN: 978-0-429-29155-5 (ebk)

Typeset in Times New Roman
by Apex CoVantage LLC

Contents

Preface x
CHRISTOPHER BOLLAS

Acknowledgements xii

Introduction 1

1 Monsters, dreams and madness: explorations in the Freudian intersubjective 7

2 An introduction to dreaming 21

3 Zombie states: reconsidering the relationship between life and death instincts 33

4 Symbiont life 47

5 Performative and enactive features of psychoanalytic witnessing: the transference as the scene of address 57

6 Silence and quiet: a phenomenology of wordlessness 73

7 Form and content 79

8 Duende and the shape of things unknown 87

9 Creative repetition 101

Index 117

In the fairytales of musicians, you are led to it
By the usual talking dog, or sloe-eyed twins
Who ask your help to dig it from the dune
Or the leaf mould. Now – in a normal story –
A faint voice snivels *if you let me out* . . .
Then rehearses its extravagant parole;
But here a solid silence is observed,
And when you've carved the block from the wet sand
Or prised it from its fist of alder-roots
To work your knife below the lid, you find
Another box, then another, and another,
And in the last, a beautiful mute bird.

'The Black Box' – Don Paterson (2005)

Preface

Bruce Reis begins his chapter on silence by distinguishing between silence and quiet. Silence in analysis is associated with the absence of speech, but quiet is a shared lived experience between analyst and patient, and gives rise to thoughtfulness. He tells us that the aim of his book is to 'explore unconscious territories', which he does in a unique way. His psychoanalytic interest is in the experience of being with others and the clinical illustrations he uses highlight the joys and the perils of residing in analytic spaces from which meaning emerges through creative events. A phenomenology of discovery, paired with a clinical approach of curiosity about experience in its varied forms, guides his explorations in memory, dreaming and fantasying aimed at finding with his patients the truths that will allow them to live more fully, relate more authentically to themselves and others and continue with the unconscious project of their individual lives.

He writes with remarkable care about the works of many contemporary analysts from differing parts of the world and divergent schools of thought. Whatever the opening topic of a chapter, he sets the stage for our experience in two distinctly different but related ways. He selects certain authors whose work he has clearly lived with for many years and as time passes he brings these differing voices into the same room. In these ways, Reis, whose own identity encompasses both European and American nationalities, brings a global sensibility to the varied traditions with which he engages. Unlike so many writers who have preceded him and feel an obligation to 'review the literature', Reis brings his selected writers into conversation with one another. In such moments, the book becomes an inspiring salon.

In reading his experience with patients, we find the same sensibility. He is a person who presents the other in highly attuned and informed ways, who brings many differing 'selves' to the table of thought and who generates a reading experience for us that is profound and seamlessly moves to discuss the patients from whom he has learned so much. His 'cases' are written up with great care and devotion. As we read them, his narrative skill conveys something of a disposition he discusses, as when he writes, 'Often I have felt swept up in an experience that feels uncanny, unbidden and ill-defined'. He cites his favourite passage from Thoreau (1980) several times – 'our truest life is when we are in dreams awake' – and reading his experience of being a psychoanalyst conveys the feel of being 'in dreams awake'.

His explorations across several chapters of the death instinct – in modern times – are compelling reading, especially when he discusses 'zombie states' as an animated deadness that beckons us all. Other chapters take up Garcia Lorca's conception of 'the Duende', linking it with contemporary theories of psychoanalytic work. He also brings his original thoughts to well-known topics, such as repetition, the relation of form to content in analytic speech and working with what has been called primitive mental states. The centrepiece of the book, however, is his chapter on 'psychoanalytic witnessing', an essay that will become a signature piece representative of psychoanalysts of his generation. He describes 'the experience of enactive witnessing'. 'I have in mind', he writes, 'an intersubjective concept that is based less on the notion of transforming an experience than transforming the patient's experience of an experience', a protean insight with ramifying implications.

We find in his work the arrival of a genuinely new voice in psychoanalysis, one that represents a new era and promises a rich future for this enigmatic profession.

There is quiet genius at work in these pages.

Christopher Bollas

Acknowledgements

I would like to acknowledge the support and friendship of colleagues who, over the years, have added immeasurably to my personal and professional lives. Several of the people mentioned next have read portions of the present book and offered their helpful advice. My affection and appreciation goes to Christopher Bollas, Lucy LaFarge, Larry Brown, Robert Grossmark, Steven Cooper, Rick Zimmer, Chris Lovett, Melinda Gellman, Jill Salberg, Jan Abram, Michael Diamond, Terry Owens, Dan Greenspun, Isaac Tylim, Mary Libby, Gil Katz, Andy Druck, Dodi Goldman, Lynn Egan, Phillip Blumberg, Gretchen Schmutz, and the past and present members of the Boston Change Process Study Group – Jeremy Nahum, Karlen Lyons-Ruth, Alec Morgan, Nadia Bruschweiler-Stern and Daniel Stern.

A group of senior colleagues deserve additional recognition for their having invited me to participate in the life of various psychoanalytic journals. These experiences have been incredibly enriching, and I thank Jay Greenberg, Lucy LaFarge, Dana Birksted-Breen and Steven Cooper. My professional communities, the New York University Postdoctoral Program in Psychotherapy and Psychoanalysis and the Institute for Psychoanalytic Training and Research, have been societies in which I have taught and learned a great deal.

To my editor, Mr. Phillip Birch, I owe a debt of gratitude for his expertise, insight and patience and to Mrs. Emily Hill Steadman whose assistance was invaluable in securing copy rite permissions I am very equally thankful.

While its cliché, I do believe that my patients have afforded me the opportunity to accompany them through their most personal challenges and successes. This book is about the unconscious relation I have shared with many of them over the years. I thank them for this and for their collective formation of me as an analyst.

It would not be possible for me to describe how important my family has been, in particular the women: my mother, my wife and my daughter have shaped the person I've become through their love, support, sensibility and creativity, and for that I am grateful beyond words and dedicate this book to them.

Copyright acknowledgements

The author and publisher gratefully acknowledge permission to reprint copyright material in this book as follows. Every effort has been made to contact the copyright holders for their permission to reprint selections of this book. The publishers would be grateful to hear from any copyright holder who is not here acknowledged, and we will undertake to rectify any errors or omissions in future editions of this book.

Chapter. 1, Bruce Reis, 'Monsters, dreams and madness: Commentary on "The arms of the chimeras"'. *The International Journal of Psychoanalysis*, Volume 97, Issue 2. A revised version of the original article published on 21 March 2016. Reprinted by permission of the publisher Taylor & Francis, LLC. (www.tandfon line.com)

Chapter. 3, Bruce Reis, 'Zombie states: Reconsidering the relationship between life and death instincts'. *Psychoanalytic Quarterly*, LXXX, Issue 2: 269–286. A revised version of the original article published on 20 December 2012. Reprinted by permission of the publisher Taylor & Francis, LLC. (www.tandfonline.com)

Chapter. 5, Bruce Reis, 'Performative enactive features of psychoanalytic witnessing: The transference as the scene of address'. the *International Journal of Psychoanalysis*, Volume 90, Issue 6. A revised version of the original article published on 09 December 2009. Reprinted by permission of the publisher Taylor & Francis, LLC. (www.tandfonline.com)

Chapter. 6, Bruce Reis, 'Silence and quiet: A phenomenology of wordlessness'. DIVISION/Review, 6: 24–26. A revised version of the original article published in 2012. Reprinted by permission of the publisher DIVISION/Review

Chapter. 9, Bruce Reis, 'Repetition & reception' as originally published in the *International Journal of Psychoanalysis*, Issue 6, 2019

Page *ix*, Don Paterson, 'The Black Box' from *Landing Light*. Copyright © 2004 by Don Paterson. Reprinted with the permission of the publisher Faber & Faber Ltd.

Page *ix*, Don Paterson, 'The Black Box' from *Landing Light*. Copyright © 2005 by Don Paterson. Reprinted with the permission of The Permissions Company, Inc., on behalf of Graywolf Press, www.graywolfpress.org

Page *1*, Jean Cocteau, *Les Mariés de la tour Eiffel* © Editions Gallimard, Paris, 1924

Page *79*, C. D. Wright, 'The old business about form & content' from The Poet, the Lion, Talking Pictures, El Farolito, A Wedding in St Roch, The Big Box Store, The Warp in the Mirror, Spring, Midnights, Fire & All. Copyright © 2015 by C. D. Wright. Reprinted with the permission of The Permissions Company, Inc. on behalf of Copper Canyon Press, www.coppercanyonpress.org

Page *87*, Federico Garcia Lorca, translated by Christopher Maurer, from In Search of Duende, copyright ©1955,1998 by New Directions Publishing Corp., Copyright © Herederos de Federico Garcia Lorca, Translation © Christopher Maurer and Hereros de Federico Garcia Lorca. Reprinted by permission of New Directions Publishing Corp.

Pages *87–88*, Tracy K. Smith, 'Survival in Two Worlds at Once: Federico Garcia Lorca and Duende', Poets.org. Reprinted by permission of the Academy of American Poets, 75 Maiden Lane, Suite 901, New York, NY 10038. https://poets.org/text/survival-two-worlds-once-federico-garcia-lorca-and-duende

Page *95*, unpublished poem by 'Ines', reprinted by permission of the poet.

Introduction

> Since these mysteries are beyond our understanding, let us pretend to rule over them.
>
> *Les Mariés de la tour Eiffel* – Jean Cocteau (1924)

Several years ago, when my daughter was still quite young, we spent a winter's day walking through the corridors of the Louvre. Having been there for a few hours, our legs weary, our attention wandered to thoughts of dinner, and we happened to turn a corner into a small room of statuary. The afternoon sunset was projected through the huge windows onto the marble walls of the room, and there, within that small space, she stopped, transfixed and utterly engaged by Antonio Canova's statue of Psyche and Eros. The object had a profound effect upon her that she did not attempt to verbalize. She found a connection with that piece over literally thousands of others we had seen that day. On our way out of the museum, we purchased a postcard of the statue that lived for many years under a glass surface on the desk in her room.

Analysis can offer a similar experience. I will meet with a person many times a week, for many years, engaged in a meandering, almost random process of association. We will look at this, then that, finding our way, partly through the use of an analytic 'map' and partly through unplanned exploration. Then we will turn a corner and something happens. Until this point, we had been doing analytic work. It was not that we were waiting for something; quite the contrary, it seemed the work was the analysis, until, of course, that corner was turned, and something else became available that wasn't so before. When Freud (1912) wrote his 'Recommendations to Physicians Practicing Psychoanalysis', he suggested a similar method of mental wandering without a predetermined aim or intention, or the deliberate concentration of attention. The most successful cases, he wrote, 'are those in which one proceeds, as it were, without any purpose in view, allows oneself to be taken by surprise by any new turn in them, and always meets them with an open mind, free from any presuppositions' (p. 114). One can immediately see how this state was placed by Bion at the centre of his notion of reverie, a 'maximally receptive state' as Birksted-Breen (2016, p. 30) described it, 'which involves not looking for anything in particular'.

'Finding' this surprising moment is necessarily predicated upon the years of work that preceded it and the nature of the engagement between analyst and analysand at deeply unconscious levels. Such events are products of that unconscious engagement and, as will be discussed at some length in this volume, take mysterious and unpredictable forms. As with the question Winnicott felt to be forbidden, we do not ask whether this experience was created or if it was found. Rather, the psychic object was there, waiting to be created by the individual or the analytic dyad. Indeed, Winnicott (1971, p. 47) came to identify the undertaking of psychoanalysis precisely as a special form of playing with this precarious issue:

> The thing about playing is always the precariousness of the interplay of personal psychic reality and the experience of control of actual objects. This is the precariousness of magic itself, magic that arises in intimacy, in a relationship that is being found to be reliable.

Analysts from different parts of the world have described this magical process of finding and creating an object in different ways: as the joint creation of intersubjective monsters (De M'Uzan, 1989), hallucinatory spaces (Botellas, 2005), dream spaces (Ogden, 2005) or making space within themselves for the patient's madness (Bollas, 1987; Searles, 1979). All of these experiences involve the analyst's regression alongside the analysand, so we see the unconscious as another dimension of human life, populating the analyst's psychic reality with monsters, dreams and madness.

Grotstein (1997) suggested the psychoanalytic concept of the 'object' to be freighted with empiricism and positivism of the Enlightenment and thus 'obsolete'. In its place, he recommended 'a return to pre-Enlightenment psychology in order to address the presence and clinical manifestation of what the term "object" screened, i.e., demons, monsters, chimera, ghosts, spirits, etc.' (p. 47). He felt these medieval conceptions to be more in keeping with the presences that haunt the unconscious than 'scientific' terms, such as 'object'. Grotstein draws our attention to the effects of Enlightenment thought on our work.[1] Like Bion before him, his approach to the unconscious attempts to free itself from Enlightenment ideals of 'knowing' and return to pre-Enlightenment modes of experiencing as an avenue to what is felt to be analytically true. Because our subject (i.e. the unconscious) is by definition unknown and will always remain so, we must not attempt to solve the paradox of its existence by searching for knowledge of it. Instead, we must be receptive to the analytic creation of meaning that occurs within the intersubjective space of the treatment as the unconscious is given shape. In this volume, I have tried to clinically and theoretically illustrate how we come close to its power only through the use of analogy, intuition, pictograms, hallucination and dreaming – all modes of 'knowing' that lay outside of the Enlightenment ideal.

Then there are 'moments' in analysis that last for years. Here I am referring not so much to a discrete event that marks the unconscious relation between analyst and analysand but the experience of time spent within that relation. Analysts know that it is misleading to focus only on what is explicitly brought into the session through the patient's material and neglect what one does not see or hear about. Indeed, the event is but the visible manifestation of an unseen process. Hours, days and years of unconscious engagement with other human beings are themselves 'events' out of any ordinary context. Periods of silence, interpretations that are taken up and others that appear to be ignored or rejected, fleeting experiences that do not rise to conscious perception for either analyst or analysand, what is made by each analytic partner of the subtle changes in the other, repeated stories, offhand comments, the way each person greets and takes leave, all when taken together form an event within psychoanalysis that often defies verbal description or goes unnoticed.

In the midst of this, an image may come to the mind of the analyst, or he may say something he hadn't intended to say, or something he did not know the meaning of when he said it. He may sit silently for long periods of time in altered states of consciousness, experiencing an unconscious aspect of the patient's mind or a seemingly minor string of personal preoccupations. Or he may experience hallucinatory flashes or somatic delusions. We must be careful not to idealize the more dramatic states that the analyst or patient may enter. These appear to us as instances of magical realism, but over-attraction to hysterical or mystical aspects of this process undermines what is at heart a deeply psychoanalytic process that also shows up as memory, intuition, fantasy and hunches over the long course of working through that constitute an analytic treatment. Technique is a central aspect of the work of every theorist I take up in this volume, and its mindful application stands in contrast to wild analysis, acting in and unreflective participation. My own work seeks to explore these unconscious territories – not only the more benign forms North American analysts tend to describe but also, and especially, the forms described by British, European and South American analysts: from Searles's 'shared madness' (1979), to South American ideas of 'vinculo' (Bernardi & De Leon De Bernardi, 2012) and shared unconscious phantasies (Baranger & Baranger, 2009), to French 'chimeras' (de M'Uzan, 1989) and hallucinations (Botella & Botella, 2005), to British ideas regarding dreamlike states (Bion, 1962). Each of these ideas, in their own way, goes beyond earlier psychoanalytic notions of the patient or analyst having an effect on the other, or simply communicating with the other. They speak instead to an unconscious intersubjective relation that subtends the content of any conscious exchange and provides the basis for a non-rational production of knowledge through non-interpretive mutative intervention, the operation of which represents the very heart of the treatment. The experiences I wish to focus on are those at the core of the individual, which may be impossible to communicate verbally, of the 'beautiful mute bird' in the box, as Paterson put it.

What I hope will strike the reader is the emphasis I place on the experiential aspect of psychoanalytic treatment, what analysts in the British tradition have referred to as the importance of the patient (and I would add the analyst) *having an experience*. The clinical vignettes I use, all of which are composite constructions or deeply disguised so as to maintain patient privacy, will not take a narrative arc so as to read like stories, because what I wish to highlight is the micro- rather than macro-level at which change occurs. Suffice it to say that my experience is that people in analysis, when they show up to do the work, almost always get better in the various developmental ways they particularly need to get better.

Whether I use concepts from contemporary Freudian or Winnicottian schools, French or South American theorists, the most salient aspect of the clinical material I present here is the experience of unconscious relation. While a piece of my analytic identity was to be trained as a relational psychoanalyst (in addition to having been trained as a contemporary Freudian), the ideas in this book are not 'relational' in the particular sense of that school's way of writing or thinking, though it is a matter of relation that is at their heart. Similarly, my intellectual commitments to the work of the French phenomenologists (particularly Merleau-Ponty and Nancy) do not show up much in these pages, but I believe they are woven into the ways in which I work and write about that work as a live encounter (cf. Alvarez, 1992). And, just as my identity is both American and European, the following pages will necessarily reflect my multiple and subjective orientations, views, perspectives and histories. Though I feel it should go without saying, while the pieces in this book focus on a particular aspect of psychoanalytic treatment, this should not be taken to mean that they represent my only approach to technique. While I concentrate on the therapeutic action of non-interpretive mutative factors, this does not mean that I believe interpretation has not been an important part of these treatments.

In the myth of Psyche and Eros, Psyche is charged with bringing a secret from the underworld, but her attempt to use the contents of what she was carrying leads her to fall into a lifeless sleep. Awakened by the kiss of Eros, Psyche is revived, and the myth ends happily. Analysts too need be careful of exposure to the unconscious processes they encounter and their ambitions in using their contents for larger analytic aims. Analysts must instead, as Freud recommended, proceed without any purpose in view and allow themselves to be surprised by any new turn. But who knows what dreams may come during the sleep of 'reverie', what monsters may appear unbidden when one ventures into this space. Our purposeless analytic wandering is a major theme of the present volume and I believe integral to the work remaining analytic. Caution is blended with analytic receptivity in each clinical description illustrating, I hope, the power of the engagement to receive the unconscious address from the other, to meet the communication and transform it as a function of the relation between analyst and analysand and, ultimately, to reawaken areas of experience for the individual that have fallen into psychic lifelessness.

Note

1 This point may be especially relevant for clinicians in North America whose practices are regularly evaluated by insurance corporations according to 'evidence-based' criteria.

References

Alvarez, A. (1992). *Live Company: Psychoanalytic Psychotherapy with Autistic, Borderline, Deprived and Abused Children.* London: Routledge.

Baranger, M. & Baranger, W. (2009). *The Work of Confluence: Listening and Interpreting in the Psychoanalytic Field.* L.G. Fiorini (Ed.). London: Karnac Books.

Bernardi, R. & De Leon De Bernardi, B. (2012). 'The Concepts of Vinculo and Dialectical Spiral: A Bridge Between Intra- and Intersubjectivity.' *Psychoanalytic Quarterly*, 81: 531–564.

Bion, W.R. (1962). *Learning from Experience.* London: Heinemann.

Birksted-Breen, D. (2016). 'Bi-ocularity, The Functioning Mind of the Psychoanalyst.' *International Journal of Psychoanalysis*, 97: 25–40.

Bollas, C. (1987). *The Shadow of the Object.* New York: Columbia University Press.

Botella, S. & Botella, C. (2005). *The Work of Psychic Figurability: Mental States Without Representation.* New York: Routledge.

Cocteau, J. (1924). *Les Mariés de la tour Eiffel.* Paris: Editions de la Nouvelle Revue Francaise.

De M'Uzan, M. (1989). 'During the Session: Considerations on the Analyst's Mental Functioning.' In: M. De M'Uzan (Ed.) *Death and Identity: Being and the Psycho-Sexual Drama.* London: Karnac Books, 2013, pp. 79–97.

Freud, S. (1912). 'Recommendations to Physicians Practicing Psycho-Analysis.' *S.E.*, Vol. 12, London: Hogarth Press, pp. 215–226.

Grotstein, J.S. (1997). '"Internal Objects" or "Chimerical Monsters"? The Demonic "Third Forms" of the Internal World.' *Journal of Analytical Psychology*, 42(1): 47–80.

Ogden, T.H. (2005). *This Art of Psychoanalysis: Dreaming Undreamt Dreams and Interrupted Cries.* New York: Routledge.

Searles, H. (1979). 'Transitional Phenomena and Therapeutic Symbiosis.' In: H. Searles (Ed.) *Countertransference.* New York: International Universities Press, 1971, pp. 503–576.

Paterson, D. (2005). 'The Black Box.' In: D. Paterson (Ed.) *Landing Light.* St. Paul, MN: Grey Wolf Press, pp. 74–80.

Winnicott, D.W. (1971). 'Playing: A Theoretical Statement.' In: D.W. Winnicott (Ed.) *Playing and Reality.* New York: Routledge, 1971, pp. 38–52.

Chapter 1

Monsters, dreams and madness
Explorations in the Freudian intersubjective

> It is true, we shall be monsters, cut off from all the world; but on that account we shall be more attached to one another.
>
> Mary Shelley, *Frankenstein* (1869, p. 115)

It seems fitting to begin this book with an examination of the Freudian and post-Freudian intersubjective approaches that will constitute a large part of its theme. Here I will introduce contemporary analytic theorists from the French, British and North American tradition, all of whom started with Freud's (1912) ideas on unconscious communication and his recommendation to analysts that they use their own unconscious 'as an instrument of the analysis' and then developed this idea well past one of communication. French analysts, such as de M'Uzan and Ithier, have concentrated on the hallucination of the analyst as an expression of the creation of the 'chimera', a monstrous hybrid of unconscious connection with their patients. The approach to the intersubjective within the British tradition has emphasized the analyst's states of 'reverie' (Bion, 1962) and will be represented in this chapter through the work of two American born analysts, Odgen and Bollas, who practice in and have extended that tradition. Perhaps most innovative in all of these approaches is the common reexamination of the issue of identity that springs from conceptualizing intersubjective exchange in terms of unconscious subjects and what their intermingling will produce.

Monsters

Within Greek mythology, the chimera is a fire-breathing creature, part goat, part lion and part serpent. Within genetic biology, the term refers to a single organism composed of two distinct sets of DNA. Quoting a 1994 text in French by de M'Uzan, Ithier introduces this concept within the analytic space:

> A new organism may emerge, that is to say, a 'psychological chimera' which has its own modes of functioning. By the very nature of their encounter, the analysand and analyst will, unwittingly, give birth to this 'fabulous child', a

powerful being, a monster 'which works in the shadows but whose growth may be affected by all influences coming from its creators'.

(Ithier, 2016, p. 455)

The emergence of de M'Uzan's chimera is dependent upon the analyst adopting a mode of 'paradoxical functioning' associated with the intertwining or interpenetration of the unconscious minds of the analyst and the analysand. De M'Uzan describes experiences in this mode, where the analyst is

> subject to a very special state of passivity; he is at the mercy of something that is happening within him . . . the analyst experiences, witnesses, lives – all words conveying the extent to which he is caught up in this aggravated state of passivity – and undergoes an inner transformation.
>
> (2013, pp. 89–90)

Within this state, the analyst may respond to something the patient hasn't said, he may experience images within his mind that feel vivid, yet which he has no feeling of responsibility for, or he may see abstract forms or faces that morph into each other. Just as suddenly and usually, after only a brief period of time, the ego may intervene so that

> words and sentences insert themselves that can undoubtedly lead to the formulation of interpretations, but also serve to help the analyst get a grip again on the consequences of passivity. The protagonists then find that acceptable boundaries have been re-established.
>
> (p. 91)

In his chapter 'Invitation to Frequent the Shadows', de M'Uzan (2006, pp. 161–162) presents several examples of clinical moments in which the boundary of identity between patient and analyst may be experienced as in flux. In a 1994 report on a more pedestrian form of this phenomenon, resulting from the paradoxical thoughts of the analyst De M'Uzan begins by observing that there was little he found especially disquieting about his patient who had been in analysis for several years. At the end of the session prior to the one he concentrates on, the patient left in an unusual way, saying to her analyst, 'Au revoir, Monsieur'. Her associations to this phrase during the next session provoked a memory that the patient had 'more or less forgotten'. The memory was from when the patient was 2-and-a-half years old and is reported as follows: She had been walking along the street when suddenly she found herself in the police station. The policemen made her stand on a table and were questioning her. In listening to the patient's memory, de M'Uzan experienced a sense of depersonalization, which he described as a background experience from which his paradoxical thoughts emerged into consciousness. Then 'an unusual thought came to my mind: *I would happily gobble you up, you handsome sailor*'. De M'Uzan did not share this surprising thought with his patient or make an interpretation, he simply noted to himself the association, which relates to Billy Budd, the hero of a Herman Melville short story he had read years before, and which he felt intuitively was connected to the 'monsieur' of the patient's farewell. Later on, he remembered that it is customary in the British or American Navy to address officers as 'sir'. As he was having these thoughts, the patient continued to recount her childhood memory. At the police station, she felt intense shame, and she stressed the peculiar quality of her experience. Then she saw her Uncle Pierre enter. The patient then shifted to talking about a dream she'd already told the analyst, but which he felt 'for some obscure reason . . . [he] wanted to hear again'. In the dream, there was a slab of stone covered in black fabric that reminded the patient of a tombstone and a table. The patient's father had once offered her a marble-topped table. The patient said she wanted to get rid of that table and replace it with another that she would choose herself: a dining table ('table à manger'). Then the patient started talking about food, telling the analyst about a local dish from her country of origin she strongly disliked: 'And yet', she insistently added, 'j'étais de bonne composition' (i.e. 'not fussy'). Once again, the analyst experienced an alteration in his thinking and without evaluating the logic of the sequences, he replied, 'In saying 'de bonne composition', perhaps you mean 'bon à manger'! ('good to eat'). Taken aback, and seemingly a little worried, the patient replied, 'Yes, it's true! I am thinking again now of that Uncle Pierre who used to frighten me so much. He used to say to me: 'I'm a lion; I'm going to eat you. I was fascinated, excited, and terrified'. The next day, de M'Uzan explored his association with Melville's character, recalling that the patient's neck had been 'conspicuously bare on that day'. Billy Budd, nicknamed the 'handsome sailor', ended up being hanged from the ship's main yard, bringing into focus the link between the tombstone and the condemned hero. De M'Uzan reported that

> at the end of this phase in the treatment, a repression with its roots in the drives and oral eroticism was lifted, in such a way that it would colour the Oedipal conflicts of the patient, in her past, and also in the actuality of her transference.

De M'Uzan writes that his experience in the session was not a countertransferential interference, as the representations that occurred 'did not depend specifically on my inner life'. According to the author, neither were they a personal reaction to the patient's transference. Instead, it was an instance in which the analyst's psychical apparatus literally became the analysand's, as it had been invaded and taken possession of so that the patient's mental process could occur there. By annexing the analyst's psychical system, the patient sought to be understood through the interposition of her representation. For his part, the analyst withdrew his individual passions and history so his functional capacities could be made use of. 'Nothing seems so convincing,' writes de M'Uzan (1999, p. 111), 'as the sudden appearance of a monster at the heart of what I have called the paraphrenic realm; and this apparition imposes itself decisively, just like a delusional idea, with incomparable clarity'.

Dreams

De M'Uzan's chimera may be compared to a form of analytic thirdness described by Ogden (1994a) as the 'subjugating third', and such a comparison has been made by Ithier (2016). Brought about through the use of projective identification, the subjugating third has the effect of subsuming within it the individual subjectivities of the participants. Important to note is the distinction between this form of thirdness and what Ogden elsewhere describes as the 'intersubjective analytic third' (1994b), which, like Green's (1975) analytic object, arises as a product of the dialectical relation between the unconscious subjective involvements of analyst and analysand. Utilizing and extending Bion's (1962) concept of 'reverie', Ogden describes his own inner transformations, resulting from dreamlike states often involving the quotidian and mundane, which lead eventually to deeper understandings of the patient and the interpretations. He writes,

> I believe that a major dimension of the analyst's psychological life in the consulting room with the patient takes the form of reverie concerning the ordinary, everyday details of his own life (that are often of great narcissistic importance to him). I have attempted to demonstrate in this clinical discussion that these reveries are not simply reflections of inattentiveness, narcissistic self-involvement, unresolved emotional conflict, and the like. Rather, this psychological activity represents symbolic and protosymbolic (sensation-based) forms given to the unarticulated (and often not yet felt) experience of the analysand as they are taking form in the intersubjectivity of the analytic pair (i.e. in the analytic third).
> (1994b, p. 82)

In the experience of the chimera, de M'Uzan writes of the analyst becoming the patient and of his need to 'withdraw[s] the most individual aspects of his personality' in order to allow himself to be 'invaded' and 'occupied' (1989 p. 84). The subjugating third that Ogden describes forming as a consequence of projective identification also involves the analyst unconsciously 'enter[ing] into a form of negation of himself as a separate I'. As he describes it, 'The recipient of the projective identification becomes a participant in the negation of himself as a separate subject, thus making "psychological room" in himself to be (in unconscious fantasy) occupied (taken over) by the projector' (p. 100). Ogden chooses words with a similar affective tenor to those de M'Uzan uses to describe this intersubjective moment, such as 'kidnapping', 'blackmailing', 'seduction', 'mesmerization', 'being swept along by the irresistible frightening lure of an unfolding horror story' (p. 105). Thus it would appear that both de M'Uzan and Ogden regard this process as a vehicle by which the analyst allows an unconscious occupation of himself so that he can experience something the patient cannot.

Madness

To the comparison of the work of de M'Uzan and Ogden I would add the work of Christopher Bollas (1987), who in an early contribution described the creation of an internal space within the analyst which can receive the patient's unconscious material. Bollas takes the view that allowing himself to 'become lost' (p. 203) in the patient's material enables a process of creation 'through transference usage into object identity' (p. 203). For this to happen, the analyst needs to be able to 'tolerate the necessary loss of his personal sense of identity within the clinical situation' (p. 203). As the patient's representation of aspects of the troubled mother, father or infant self are experienced by the analyst, he allows a part of himself to become 'disturbed' by the patient and 'situationally ill' (p. 204), staying 'receptive to varying degrees of "madness" in myself occasioned by life in the patient's environment' (p. 204). In more recent work, Bollas continues his earlier emphasis on the unconscious dimensions of intersubjective exchange, painting psychoanalysis as an unconscious object relation. He writes, 'Even as an unconscious subject I am still shaped by another's effect on me. My self is given a new form by the *other*' (1995, p. 25, my italics). The analyst's access to this level of exchange occurs through 'a form of intersubjectivity that assumes unconscious perception, unconscious organization, unconscious creativity and unconscious communication' (2001, p. 95). Bollas places both patient and analyst within the dream space where this relation occurs:

> Freud's unconscious receiver, the dream set of counter-transference, processes the patient's unconscious communications on its own terms: one dreamer to another. Dreaming the analysand during the hour, bringing the patient to another place, transformed into other persons, events, and places, the analyst *unconsciously* deconstructs – displaces, condenses, substitutes the patient.
>
> (1995, p. 12)

These three clinical psychoanalytic approaches are predicated on innovative understandings of identity. For each of these theorists, their ability to move into the psychic spaces they describe relies on their use of Freudian and post-Freudian thought to ground their original technical contributions. By appreciating the unique approach each theorist takes to the issue of identity, one may better appreciate the novel clinical approaches they have introduced.

New approaches to identity

Comparing de M'Uzan with Ogden and Bollas brings us to the issue of the foundational changes each has envisioned with regard to the notion of identity. At the heart of their approaches is a revised Freudian understanding of this notion that allows clinicians to go to the psychic places their patients take them. It is interesting to note that one finds similar notions in the work of Searles (1979, p. 508), who wrote of using his own 'sense of identity as a perceptual organ' in the treatment of schizophrenic, borderline and neurotic patients by entering states of therapeutic symbiosis with them.

According to de M'Uzan (1978), the ego is not entirely encompassed within the 'I', nor entirely in the 'other'. There is no fixed boundary between the domains of the ego and non-ego but, instead, a transitional area,[1] a *spectrum of identity* that is defined by the set of diverse positions narcissistic libido can occupy – what he has called a 'zone of *floating individuation*' (1983, p. 61). De M'Uzan plays with Freud's notions of opposition and balance between narcissistic libido and object libido by allowing narcissistic libido to exist in multiple locations simultaneously. By moving narcissistic libido out of the province of the 'I', de M'Uzan allows object experience to be suffused with what might be called external narcissistic libido. He writes,

> The narcissistic libido is not characterized by total localization within the subject . . . We have seen how the object, while gradually establishing itself, retains a part of the subject as well as part of its original libidinal cathexis . . . It is thus no longer necessary to say that the more libido the object absorbs, the more the narcissistic libido diminishes.
>
> (1978, pp. 489–490)

Along this spectrum of identity, de M'Uzan locates our psychic life amongst others. Thus he writes,

> Just as 'I' cannot pass completely to the other without annihilating itself, it cannot withdraw utterly from the object without transforming the latter into a mass of abstract and meaningless elements. It is not the amount of object-libido invested in the external world that gives things their familiar aspect, but the fragment of narcissistic libido retained by these objects and establishing, as it were, the extra-territorial rights of the 'I', and serving as the subject's vanguard.
>
> (1978, p. 490)

Ogden makes analogous conceptual moves when redefining the psychoanalytic subject as being dialectically constituted and decentred. He begins (1994c) by situating the Freudian analytic subject not in the ego but as dispersed within the dialectical interplay of consciousness and unconsciousness. Ogden reads Klein, Bion and Rosenfeld as proposing views of the subject within the concept of projective identification that are 'interpersonally decentered from its exclusive locus within the individual' (1994d, p. 47). Further building on Winnicott's statement that there is no such thing as an infant, Ogden continues to expand his concept of the decentred subject within Winnicott's intersubjective scheme, understanding the subject to be always decentred from itself and always to some degree arising in the context of intersubjectivity. This move allows Ogden to approach the psychoanalytic subject as 'forever decentered from static self-equivalence . . . the subject is always *becoming* through a process of the creative negation of itself' (1994e, p. 60).

The issue of identity is similarly elusive for Bollas (2011), who, after emphasizing a uniqueness of the personality, an 'idiom', goes on to write about how that idiom gains shape and expression via objects encountered. Like de M'Uzan and Ogden, Bollas writes of the individual immersed in fluid processes of unconscious exchange with objects and others, processes which unhinge but do not do away with the certain oppositions of self and other, internal and external. Subjects for him are like ineffable spirits who move unconsciously through each other, creating personal experiences in the process and leaving their traces.

In his book, *Being a Character* (1992), Bollas describes it thusly:

> As we move through the object world, breathing our life into the impersonal, we gather and organize our personal effects. As we collide with other subjectivities, we exchange differing syntheses, and leave the other with his or her inner senses of our self, just as we carry the spirit of the other's idiom within our unconscious . . . And of ourselves, I think it can be said that we are spirits, that we shall scatter our being throughout the object world, and through the winds of interforming human mutualities.
>
> (p. 65)

With a similarity to de M'Uzan's description of the floating zone of individuation, Bollas (1995) writes of moving through the object world and 'disseminating' oneself, one's being, into and through that world via one's encounters with people and things, at the same time that people and things are used by the individual to give form to one's own idiom. Like de M'Uzan, Bollas describes the narcissistic use that the subject makes of the object, and he also considers the effect on the subject as a result of engaging with the world this way – a change that he makes central to his clinical approach. For Bollas, the objects we choose evoke and rearrange us, break us up in different ways, and open the self just as keys open a lock. Through this inevitable sculpting of subjective experience, we are constantly being changed (opened up, divided, put together differently) via our interaction, our collision with what can be considered the 'intelligent breeze of the other who moves through us, to affect us, shaping within us the ghost of that spirit when it is long gone' (Bollas, 1992, p. 63).

The ways in . . .

It is striking to note the ways in which analysts describe the process of entering the unconscious psychic spaces they occupy with their patients. Common to all their experiences appears to be an initial unconscious receptivity to be contacted, used or taken over. For de M'Uzan, an extreme depersonalization occurs. Perhaps akin to an experience of possession, de M'Uzan's depersonalization seems to go beyond the interpenetration of unconscious minds. As Ithier (2016) describes it, 'the analyst is prepared to experience a certain vacillation of his/her identity by moving in a territory where ego and not-ego lose their differences and their contours'. She observes a difference between de M'Uzan and Ogden in that the former's conception of the intersubjective 'affects the whole of the analyst's subjective territory and not just one of its aspects'.

To my mind, it seems difficult to say which portions of the analyst's subjective territory are affected and which are not, especially in light of de M'Uzan's caution that the analyst's 'I' cannot pass completely to the other without annihilating itself; Ogden's notion of the subjugating third involving the negation of the analyst's identity as he 'makes psychological room' to be occupied and taken over by the patient, and Bollas's understanding that his experience of self is given form by the patient's unconscious. Seen from a Bionian (1970) position, all three approaches involve transformations in 'O' as the analyst alters his ego, in whole or part, for an experience of at-one-ment.

Experiencing these phenomena in my own work (Reis, 2011a), I have found it difficult to draw clear distinctions between dream, hallucination, creative seizure and depersonalization. Often, I have felt swept up in an experience that feels uncanny, unbidden and ill defined. It seems to me that all of these descriptions are experiences of the same sort of contact, whether brief or extended, considered to be primarily unconscious to preconscious or conscious to preconscious. All involve the internal transformation of the analyst as a function of his unconscious receptivity. It would be surprising to me if analysts who were open to such experiences found themselves limited to one version of this phenomenon but not another (e.g. reverie but not hallucination, chimera but not situational illness). Having taken seriously Freud's (1912) recommendation to use the unconscious 'as an instrument of the analysis', colleagues worldwide have developed a variety of complex and elegant approaches, inflected by their own regional styles and personal signatures (Ferro & Civitarese, 2015; Baranger & Baranger, 2009; Brown, 2011; Bolognini, 2011; Diamond, 2014; Roussillon, 2011; Suchet, 2004; Botella & Botella, 2005; Grotstein, 2000; Eshel, 2013 – to make only a partial list).

This chapter opens a discussion on varied approaches to the Freudian intersubjective, a discussion that includes a rich array of creative approaches to the analyst's use of his or her unconscious. This conversation highlights how a long-standing debate between one-person and two-person psychologies that has occurred in North America limits full appreciation of the unconscious aspects of intersubjective exchange by creating a stifling dichotomization that diverts focus from this level of contact. For de M'Uzan, Ogden and Bollas, the focus is not on one subjectivity or another, or even on a relationship between the two, but on unconscious processes occurring between themselves and their patients as fluid exchanges of being and becoming, wherein analyst becomes patient, new subjects are created through shared dreams and through which monsters appear.

Chimeras, traumatic and fanciful

In describing her analysis with an aggressive patient, Claude, who suffered from feelings of abandonment and a lack of warmth, Ithier (2016, p. 468) reported an uncanny and unusual experience that occurred out of the blue. Drawing on several of de M'Uzan's conceptualizations, such as the instant of seizure and the vital identical, Ithier develops her own conceptualization of the chimera within the realm of traumatic affinity between patient and analyst. Sitting with Claude, she wrote,

> I felt suddenly transformed into a cow or, to be more precise, I felt I had become a cow. This 'chimera' did not fail to intrigue me. Claude came four times a week. After the event, I thought about the milk of the four udders. I wondered about the style of my interventions and the digestion in the stomachs of the sessions of the projections and reproaches that peppered them. This image did not fail to astonish me until the day when Claude told me that as a little girl, her mother, a farmer's daughter, used to go and seek comfort from a cow after her mother's death . . . It was only later, as I was reflecting constantly on the appearance of this 'chimera' in the treatment, that I remembered a cow that I had chosen at a time when I was separated from my mother during the summer when I was two years old, a cow that I would call out to and find again with joy, saying, 'there you are my cow!', as I went to fetch milk at the farm with my grandmother. I understood that this 'chimera', arising from the resonance of our unconscious minds or rather from that of the traumatic zones of our certain structural homology between the traumatic situation of her mother losing her own mother and my situation when my mother was absent. It was as if, in the elaboration of her projective identifications, I had drawn on my helpful cow which I had used that year to bring back the primary mother, and had shared it with Claude and her internal mother.

I find that Ithier's (2016) use of the chimera makes recognizable traumatic areas of experience between analysand and analyst, what she terms their 'traumatic affinities'. She describes the unconscious links that arise from the respective traumatic zones of patient and analyst, deployed in the here and now of the session, predominately in vibrant, sensorial, affective and emotional forms, 'in what is almost a motor address to the analyst'. These are similar to what I have described (Reis, 2009a) as 'enactive memory phenomena', though I see these occurring in continuous ways in addition to their more striking appearances as discrete events:

> As an enactive phenomenon this happening is experienced as an intensity of traumatic activation, and not yet as a content. The memory is the action, the affective reactivation of the body, rather than referring to the content of an experience. It is similar to what Klein (1957, 1961) called 'memories in feelings'; and may be thought as experience's immanence in the immediacy of non-conscious affective exchange between patient and analyst.

I link these phenomena to the creation of an address to the analyst, a communication within the performative and motoric dimensions of the transference-countertransference that conveys experience beyond the human ability to grasp or imagine symbolically, yet allows patient and analyst together to have an experience of witnessing.

Ithier's description of traumatic links between analyst and patient also puts me in mind of the work of Davoine and Gaudilliere (2004) into the 'social link' between patient and analyst mitigating the effect of actual social history on individual madness. Like Ithier, these authors also describe utterances the analyst had no intention of speaking and the transformations of analyst and patient into characters from the patient's history as they link to events from the history of the analyst:

> At these times when he is somehow *touché*, as they say in fencing, the analyst is caught up in the catastrophic area of the investigation. Subject and object are confused: here and there, inside and outside. The past is present, the dead return. It is a child's voice that is speaking, in a session, through the mouth of the adult he has become, in the name of an entire society threatened with disappearance. Killings on the far-off African shores take up residence in a massacre that occurred in the mountains where the analyst was born, at the same time or years earlier.
>
> (2004, p. xxviii)

Similar to the work of Davoine and Gaudilliere, I would regard Ithier's extension of the chimera to these traumatic realms as a special genus of monster and differentiate it from de M'Uzan's as she does. Quoting de M'Uzan, Ithier describes her version of the chimera as 'proceeding from little 'hallucinations', in which the fanciful plays a major part' ('ou le Romanesque, joue a plein') where her own version 'arises from the unconscious encounter of the traumatic traces in the emotional furrows of the analyst' (Ithier, 2016, p. 476). Here the word 'fanciful', also possibly translated as 'unrealistic' or 'fictional', is quite important as it returns us to the analyst fully feeling or fully inhabiting the dream space. Ithier makes use of the imaginative component of this dream space in her work with the three patients presented and her deployment of 'a metaphorical interpretative modality' (Ithier, 2016, p. 462).

Fanciful and traumatic differences also exist in the analyst's orientation towards self and the nature of analytic experiencing. Working in the zone of traumatic affinities, rather than losing him or herself, the analyst is more likely to enact (i.e. find) unknown aspects of him or herself or of his or her own history within the transference-countertransference (Reis, 2005). Of course, the division between the areas is not clean, and unconscious communication is to varying degrees infused with traumatic nodes. The relation between these areas will always be a matter of degrees and what will be crucial is the analyst knowing enough to navigate both situations differently. A clear hazard concerns the change from working in the realm of multiple realities marked by essential uncertainties (Kohon, 1999) and the virtue accorded by Eigen (2011) to 'unknowing', to construction of concretized narrative understandings claiming a single authority.

A final note on epistemologies and ontologies

Returning to the issue of how much of the analyst's subjective experience is affected by the patient's unconscious influence, it seems important to note that the answer will partly depend on the epistemic and ontological commitments of the psychoanalyst. Bion's approach was grounded in the empirical and intellectualist views of Locke and Kant, who themselves carried forward the Cartesian idea that perception is an internal (mental) representation of an external material world built of sensations. Thus in Bion's conception of beta elements as atomistic sense data, meaningless elements that serve as the building blocks of complex internal perceptions, we find an approach both abstract and dualistic – abstract because our representations are taken to be endlessly derivative experiences of an unknowable reality and dualistic because bodily sensation is split from the mental operations that are thought to yield experience and representation. I have argued (Reis, 2006, 2010a) that the empiricist-intellectualist grounding of this approach has limited an appreciation of its intersubjective potential and has suggested instead (Reis, 1999a, 1999b, 2007, 2009b, 2010b, 2011b) a different basis in non-representational phenomenology which may better support such conceptualizations. To this end, I remain interested in the ways phenomenologies developed by Merleau-Ponty (1962), Husserl (1960), Heidegger (1962), Jean-Luc Nancy (2000) and others may be applied to our understandings of phenomena, such as unconscious communication, and to new Freudian approaches to identity.

Ithier (2016) ends her comparative essay by quoting Mallarme (1895, p. 188) on the chimera's agony, its

> combination of the motifs that compose a logic' represented so well in her comparison of the work of de M'Uzan and Ogden, and by her own extension into the realm of traumatic affinities. As a beginning to this volume the complex conceptualizations of monsters, dreams and madness offered here all clearly begin in a Freudian approach to working with the unconscious and will serve as the opening to a discussion that through this book will develop into varied and at times contrasting intersubjective ideas and approaches. My hope is that this discussion, which is only at its beginning stages, will draw even more attention to the unconscious intersubjective relation in psychoanalytic work and to the strains of its 'melodic encipherment'.
> (Mallarme, 1895, p. 188)

Note

1 De M'Uzan (1999) differentiates his ideas regarding a transitional area from those of Winnicott by emphasizing in his notion the importance of the displacements of narcissistic cathexis of representations rather than external reality.

References

Baranger, M. & Baranger, W. (2009). *The Work of Confluence: Listening and Interpreting in the Psychoanalytic Field.* L.G. Fiorini (Ed.). London: Karnac Books.
Bion, W.R. (1962). *Learning from Experience.* New York: Basic Books.
Bion, W.R. (1970). *Attention and Interpretation.* London: Heinemann.
Bollas, C. (1987). 'Expressive Uses of the Countertransference.' In: *The Shadow of the Object.* New York: Columbia University Press, pp. 200–235.
Bollas, C. (1992). *Being a Character.* New York: Hill and Wang.
Bollas, C. (1995). *Cracking Up: The Work of Unconscious Experience.* New York: Hill and Wang.
Bollas, C. (2001). 'Freudian Intersubjectivity: Commentary on Paper by Julie Gerhardt and Annie Sweetnam.' *Psychoanalytic Dialogues*, 11: 93–105.
Bollas, C. (2011). 'Character and Interformality.' In: *The Christopher Bollas Reader*, New York: Routledge, pp. 238–248.
Bolognini, S. (2011). *Secret Passages: The Theory and Technique of Interpsychic Relations.* New York: Routledge.
Botella, S. & Botella, C. (2005). *The Work of Psychic Figurability: Mental States Without Representation.* New York: Routledge.
Brown, L.J. (2011). *Intersubjective Processes and the Unconscious.* New York: Routledge.
Davoine, F. & Gaudilliere, J.M. (2004). *History Beyond Trauma.* New York: Other Books.
De M'Uzan, M. (1978). 'If I Were Dead.' *International Review of Psycho-Analysis*, 5: 485–490.
De M'Uzan, M. (1989). 'During the Session: Considerations on the Analyst's Mental Functioning.' In: *Death and Identity: Being and the Psycho-Sexual Drama.* London: Karnac Books, 2013, pp. 79–97.
De M'Uzan, M. (1994). 'La bouche de l'Inconscient.' In: *La bouche de l'Inconscient.* Paris: Gallimard, pp. 33–44.
De M'Uzan, M. (1999). 'The Paraphrenic Twin or at the Frontiers of Identity.' In: *Death and Identity: Being and the Psycho-Sexual Drama.* London: Karnac Books, 2013, pp. 101–118.
De M'Uzan, M. (2006). 'Invitation to Frequent the Shadows.' In: *Death and Identity.* London: Karnac Books, pp. 147–165.
Diamond, M.J. (2014). 'Analytic Mind Use and Interpsychic Communication: Driving Force in Analytic Technique, Pathway to Unconscious Mental Life.' *Psychoanalytic Quarterly*, 83: 525–563.
Eigen, M. (2011). *Contact with the Depths.* London: Karnac Books.
Eshel, O. (2013). 'Patient-Analyst "Withness": On Analytic "Presencing," Passion, and Compassion in States of Breakdown, Despair, and Deadness.' *Psychoanalytic Quarterly*, 82(4): 925–963.
Ferro, A. & Civitarese, G. (2015). *The Analytic Field and Its Transformations.* London: Karnac Books.
Freud, S. (1912). 'Recommendations to Physicians Practicing Psycho-Analysis.' *S.E.*, Vol. 12, London: Hogarth Press, pp. 215–226.
Green, A. (1975). 'The Analyst, Symbolization and Absence in the Analytic Setting (On Changes in Analytic Practice and Analytic Experience).' *International Journal of Psychoanalysis*, 56: 1–22.

Grotstein, J.S. (2000). *Who Is the Dreamer, Who Dreams the Dream? A Study of Psychic Presences*. Hillsdale, NJ: Analytic Press.
Heidegger, M. (Ed.) (1962). *Being and Time*. New York: Harper & Row.
Husserl, D. (1960). *Cartesian Meditations: An Introduction to Phenomenology*. D. Cairns (Ed.). The Hague: Martinus Nijhoff.
Ithier, B. (2016). 'The Arms of the Chimera.' *International Journal of Psychoanalysis*, 97: 451–478.
Klein, M. (1957). 'Envy and Gratitude.' In: *The Writings of Melanie Klein*, Vol. 3. London: Hogarth, 1975, pp. 176–235.
Klein, M. (1961). 'Narrative of Child Analysis.' In: *The Writings of Melanie Klein*, Vol. 4. London: Hogarth, 1975.
Kohon, G. (1999). *No Lost Certainties to Be Recovered*. London: Karnac Books.
Mallarme, S. (1895). 'Music and Letters.' In: B. Johnson (Trans.) *Divagations*. Cambridge, MA: Harvard University Press, 2007.
Merleau-Ponty, C. (1962). *The Phenomenology of Perception*. C. Smith (Ed.). New York: Routledge (Original work published 1945).
Nancy, J.L. (2000). *Being Singular Plural*. Stanford, CA: Stanford University Press.
Ogden, T.H. (1994a). 'Projective Identification and the Subjugating Third.' In: *Subjects of Analysis*. Northvale, NJ: Jason Aronson, pp. 97–106.
Ogden, T.H. (1994b). 'The Analytic Third: Working with Intersubjective Clinical Facts.' In: *Subjects of Analysis*. Northvale, NJ: Jason Aronson, pp. 61–95.
Ogden, T.H. (1994c). 'The Freudian Subject.' In: *Subjects of Analysis*. Northvale, NJ: Jason Aronson, pp. 13–31.
Ogden, T.H. (1994d). 'Toward an Intersubjective Conception of the Subject: The Kleinian Contribution.' In: *Subjects of Analysis*. Northvale, NJ: Jason Aronson, pp. 33–48.
Ogden, T.H. (1994e). 'Winnicott's Intersubjective Subject.' In: *Subjects of Analysis*. Northvale, NJ: Jason Aronson, pp. 49–60.
Reis, B. (1999a). 'Thomas Ogden's Phenomenological Turn.' *Psychoanalytic Dialogues*, 9: 371–393.
Reis, B. (1999b). 'Adventures of the Dialectic.' *Psychoanalytic Dialogues*, 9: 407–414.
Reis, B. (2005). 'The Subject of History/The Object of Transference.' *Studies in Gender and Sexuality*, 6: 217–240.
Reis, B. (2006). 'Even Better Than the Real Thing.' *Contemporary Psychoanalysis*, 42: 177–196.
Reis, B. (2007). 'Sensing and (Analytic) Sensibilities: Some Thoughts Following Eyal Rozmarin's "An Other in Psychoanalysis".' *Contemporary Psychoanalysis*, 43: 374–385.
Reis, B. (2009a). 'Performative and Enactive Features of Psychoanalytic Witnessing: The Transference as the Scene of Address.' *International Journal of Psycho-Analysis*, 90: 1359–1372.
Reis, B. (2009b). 'We: Commentary on Papers by Trevarthen, Ammaniti & Trentini, and Gallese.' *Psychoanalytic Dialogues*, 19: 565–579.
Reis, B. (2010a). 'Enactive Fields: An Approach to Interaction in the Kleinian-Bionian Model: Commentary on Paper by Lawrence J. Brown.' *Psychoanalytic Dialogues*, 20: 695–703.
Reis, B. (2010b). 'A Human Family: Commentary on Paper by Elisabeth Fivaz-Depeursinge, Chloe Lavanchy-Scaiola and Nicolas Favez.' *Psychoanalytic Dialogues*, 20: 151–157.

Reis, B. (2011a). 'Zombie States: Reconsidering the Relationship between Life and Death Instincts.' *Psychoanalytic Quarterly*, LXXX: 269–286.
Reis, B. (2011b). 'Reading Kohut Through Husserl.' *Psychoanalytic Inquiry*, 31: 75–83.
Roussillon, R. (2011). 'Drives and Intersubjectivity.' In: *Primitive Agony and Symbolization*. London: Karnac Books, pp. 29–48.
Searles, H. (1979). 'Transitional Phenomena and Therapeutic Symbiosis.' In: *Countertransference*. New York: International Universities Press, pp. 503–576.
Shelley, M.W. (1869). *Frankenstein or The Modern Prometheus*. Boston: Sever, Francis & Co.
Suchet, M. (2004). 'Whose Mind Is It Anyway?' *Studies in Gender and Sexuality*, 5: 259–287.

Chapter 2
An introduction to dreaming

> Our truest life is when we are in dreams awake.
> Henry David Thoreau, *A week on the Concord and Merrimack Rivers* (1980, p. 297)

Consider the science fiction movie *Arrival* (2016). The aliens are so different from the humans. They have different forms, are unnervingly mysterious and communicate in a language we can't comprehend. Over the course of the movie, a human character begins to have strange experiences; she has dreams or hallucinations related to situations and people in her own life, but somehow she knows these dreams are related to the experience of encountering the aliens. Contact is made, but it is made through the deepest layers of the human, of being human, inside a person's history, in a way that creates hitherto unknown meaning and affect. In this contact, a condensation occurs between the alien and the receiver's mind such that a new psychic presence is formed, and the receiver 'becomes' this transformation of the alien's projected mind. I use this analogy to describe the unconscious life of the other, which is contacted and encountered by the analyst in the deepest and most profoundly human manner.

A Freudian beginning

All contemporary psychoanalytic approaches to dreaming in the clinical situation follow Freud's writing on the unconscious. The variations in different theorist's conceptualizations are essentially variations on a theme, with each theorist choosing to emphasize a part of Freud's thinking other theorists often include but do not make central. The effect is to produce several analytic theories of the distinction between waking thought and dreaming that bear strong resemblance to each other but differ in some interesting and important ways.

In his 'Recommendations to Physicians' (1912), Freud made the famous suggestion that the analyst should

> turn his own unconscious like a receptive organ toward the transmitting unconscious of the patient. He must adjust himself to the patient as a telephone

receiver is adjusted to the transmitting microphone. Just as the receiver converts back into sound waves the electrical oscillations in the telephone line which were set up by sound waves, so the doctor's unconscious is able, from the derivatives of the unconscious which are communicated to him, to reconstruct that unconscious, which has determined the patient's free associations.

(pp. 115–116)

Larry Brown (2011, p. 20) considers this quotation the 'big bang' moment in the psychoanalytic universe, the moment that kicked off a century of investigation into intersubjective processes and the unconscious. The subjective experience of the dreamer was described by Freud in *The Interpretation of Dreams* (1900). There he suggested that the dreamer does not experience thoughts but instead, 'a complete hallucinatory cathexis of the perceptual systems' (p. 548). Freud emphasized the distinction between waking thought and dreaming by writing that the dream work is 'completely different from [waking thought] and for that reason not immediately comparable with it' (p. 507). Later, in his paper 'The Unconscious' (1915), he again considered these differences, suggesting of the dream that 'thought is represented as an immediate situation with the "perhaps" omitted ... transformed into visual images and speech'. He concluded that we may expect to find these characteristics 'in processes that belong to the system Ucs.' (p. 187).

A year after publishing his 'Recommendations for Physicians', Freud (1913) returned to the issue of technique. In 'On Beginning the Treatment', he wrote, 'while I am listening to the patient, I, too, give myself over to the current of my unconscious thoughts' (p. 134). And a few years later, again in his paper 'The Unconscious' (1915), he would write about the phenomenon of one person receiving another person's unconscious without it passing through his consciousness – that is to say, without preconscious intermediation. Here he brought in the topics that are of interest to us today, writing that

> unconscious processes only become cognizable (we would now probably say 'mentalized' [Fonagy et al., 2004]) by us under the conditions of dreaming and of neurosis – that is to say, when processes of the higher Pcs. system are set back to an earlier stage (by regression). In themselves they cannot be cognized.
>
> (1915, p. 186)

When motor discharge is blocked, these processes, he wrote, may also not be mentalized as reflective thought but concrete imagistic perceptions that he called hallucinatory.

In his 1923 encyclopaedia article 'Psycho-Analysis', Freud summarized,

> Experience soon showed that the attitude which the analytic physician could most advantageously adopt was to surrender himself to his own unconscious mental activity, in a state of evenly suspended attention, to avoid so far as

possible reflection and the construction of conscious expectations, not to try to fix anything that he heard particularly in his memory, and by these means to catch the drift of the patient's unconscious with his own unconscious.

(p. 239)

Finally, in his 1922 paper 'Dreams and Telepathy', he wrote that telepathic dreams are 'a perception of something external, in relation to which the mind remains passive and receptive' (p. 208). If telepathy did exist, Freud said that it would most likely appear in a dreamlike state of mind.

Keep in mind these themes: dreaming and hallucination as a conduit to unconscious experience, regression leading to earlier forms of thinking and perceiving and the unconscious of one person being received by the unconscious of another. The dream and the hallucination continue to be seen as reliable conduits to the patient's unconscious experience by analysts who allow themselves to enter spaces of psychic regression in parallel to their patient's process. But now these terms take on additional meanings as we consider the analyst to be dreaming in the session alongside his patient or hallucinating a piece of his patient's unrepresented inner world while he himself is in a regressed state.

A first variation

Bion's approach to dreaming in the analytic hour is well known and has been adopted and expanded by numerous other theorists (Ogden, 2005; Ferro, 2017; Brown, 2011). For Bion, dreaming served a very particular function. According to Grotstein (1997), 'Bion replaced Freud's concepts of the id, the unconscious, and the 'seething cauldron', with an epistemic function that harkens back to the creative role of the unconscious in the construction of dreams and jokes'. It was in this way, Bion believed, that the mind gives meaning to emotional experience. According to Schneider (2010), the task of dreaming for Bion is to work on the events, the 'facts' of lived experience. Schneider (2010) writes, 'Bion believes that dreaming is thinking about emotional experience and that, in the process of dreaming, conscious lived experience is made available to the unconscious for psychological work'. Dreaming is the way a mother transforms experiences for her infant from raw unmediated sensory phenomena into unconscious experience that can be tolerated and linked to other unconscious experience, which can eventually be thought. The mother's reverie modifies raw experience for the infant, thereby performing a containing function for unprocessed emotional experiences. Ogden (1994) expanded Bion's original conception of *reverie* as an active receptivity to 'a motley collection of psychological states that seem to reflect the analyst's narcissistic self-absorption, obsessional rumination, day-dreaming, sexual fantasizing, and so on'.

Through dreaming, meaning is made of raw experience, and if we weren't able to dream (or if someone else was not helping us do it), we would be faced with an inner world dominated by psychotic dimensions. Bion introduced the idea that dreaming is not simply a night-time activity but also a process which makes sense of our waking experience. Night-time dreaming for Bion operates under the aegis of the pleasure principle, whereas waking dream thoughts, or *reverie*, operate under the reality principle, in that reveries give meaning to the reality of our emotions.

We transform raw emotional experience into something that can be thought and felt, something which can be given meaning, and we do this by applying our ability to dream, by which Bion meant the waking application of alpha function to the raw experiences. While Bion wrote of the *inability* to dream in psychotic individuals, contemporary analysts have expanded the notion to encompass *blocked* dreaming in non-psychotic individuals who suffer from inchoate and early traumatic experience that have never been processed. As Ogden (2007) described,

> Undreamable experience may have its origins in trauma – unbearably painful emotional experience such as the early death of a parent, the death of a child, military combat, rape or imprisonment in a death camp. But undreamable experience may also arise from 'intrapsychic trauma'.

Here he is referring to experiences of being overwhelmed by conscious and unconscious fantasies. The latter form may stem from the failure of the mother to adequately hold the infant and contain his primitive anxieties, or from a constitutional psychic fragility that renders the individual in infancy and childhood unable to dream his emotional experience, even with the help of a 'good-enough' mother (Winnicott, 1958). Undreamable experience – whether it be the consequence of predominantly external or intrapsychic forces – remain with the individual in the form of undreamt dreams – i.e. psychosomatic illness, split-off psychosis, 'disaffected' states (McDougall, 1984), pockets of autism (Tustin, 1981), severe perversions (de M'Uzan, 2003) and addictions.

Following Bion's notion quite closely, Odgen (2005) considers 'the differentiation of, and interplay between unconscious and conscious life [to be] created by – not simply reflected in – dreaming'. It is this that he feels 'makes us human', and its failure strands us in states where it is impossible to tell the difference between unconscious psychic constructions and waking perceptions. Ogden writes about this in terms of the patient's need to dream himself into being, to exist in a more fully alive way by being able to create emotional meaning through dreaming his lived emotional experience.

Bion's model shifts our emphasis from the content of thought to the circumstances of breakdown in the capacity for thought. Ogden (2007) put it elegantly when he wrote,

> Just as Winnicott shifted the focus of analytic theory and practice from play (as a symbolic representation of the child's internal world) to the experience of playing, Bion shifted the focus from the symbolic content of thoughts to the process of thinking, and from the symbolic meaning of dreams to the process of dreaming.

An implication of Bion's use of dreaming is to transform psychoanalysis into a process approach in which symbolization and its failure are accorded a more central role in contemporary thinking and become more intimately related to the importance of lived experience. 'Instead of a psychoanalysis of contents and memories', Ferro (2009) writes, this approach produces, 'a psychoanalysis that gives priority to the development of the apparatus for dreaming, feeling, and thinking'. Yet Wilson (2018) warns that such a priority 'can too easily lead the analyst to overvalue his or her own ideas and feelings and mistake them for the patient's experience'. This risk is substantial, writes Wilson, who invokes the Bionian question: When is a 'selected fact' merely an 'over-valued idea' (Britton & Steiner, 1994)?

A second variation

The French analytic couple, the Botellas, have described the analyst's 'hallucinations' in their clinical work, but to think about this concept properly, we must begin with an appreciation of 'The Work of the Negative' by Andre Green (1998) in which he reminded the reader that the negative is present in Freud's 'basic assumptions'. As Green read Freud's account of the development of the ego, he highlighted the idea of the negative as a prerequisite for psychic development, writing, 'It is because of the lack of the object under the pressure of the drives seeking satisfaction that the mind is activated and gives birth to the wish hallucinatory fulfilment that constitutes the most elementary form of psychic activity'. Like Freud, both Winnicott and Bion would later emphasize the role of the absent other in the constitution of the psyche, and Green follows in this tradition by proposing that the negative hallucination 'creates a potential space for the representation and investment of new objects and the conditions in which the activities of thinking and symbolization can take place' (Perelberg, 2016).

Green's rather revolutionary technical proposal, presented in 'The Analyst, Symbolization and Absence in the Analytic Setting (on Changes in Analytic Practice and Analytic Experience)' at the 1975 IPA meetings, suggested that

> analysts lend themselves to the fusional needs of their [non-neurotic] patients while the focus is on the force of the negative – destructive mental states where connection is superseded by disconnections that in turn lead to disorganization resulting in blank depression and negative hallucination.
> (Reed, 2015)

Such states call upon the analyst to transform the inner experiences evoked within him or herself into words. Thus by using the analyst's own representational capacities, Green (1975) wrote that analysts 'enter a world . . . which requires imagination' with the aim of 'binding . . . the inchoate and containing it *within a form*' (my emphasis).

The work of the Botellas (2005) follows Green in that they have been interested in the *analyst's* difficulties in thinking, which they believe point to phenomena in the patient beyond memory and representation. The Botellas have studied 'the unforeseen, unexpected relaxations, drops in the tension of thinking, [that take] the ego by surprise, in spite of itself' (p. 122). Emphasizing Freud's attitude of passivity and reception they contrast their approach with that of Bion, who they view as applying 'an active, strong attitude of the analyst's ego'. Their interest instead is

> in the ruptures in the analyst's habitual psychic work, facilitated by the regression of his thinking; in the 'accidents' occurring in the course of his thinking marking temporary pauses in the connections of free association. These are 'flaws' in the thick tissue of the bindings and investment of ideas that open the analysis up to a work of transformation, of figurability.' For the Botellas these flaws also open to an experience of the analyst's non-pathological hallucination during the session.

As explained by Luciane Falcão (2017), the Botellas introduced the notion of the hallucinatory outside of psychiatric connotations, as a metapsychological conception:

> Their aim was to extend the scope of a theory excessively centered on the notion of representation, and thus insufficient to explain certain analytic structures and processes. To those authors, the hallucinatory [is] at the foundation of a transformational dynamic of representation-perception-hallucination, a continuing psychic process, the kinetic representation of the drive as impulse (Drang) and movement. A process that is inseparable from the path of regredience developed through dreams.

Seen as a product of the analyst's regression, the potential for hallucinatory expression in dream states is also viewed by the Botellas (2005, p. 127) to exist outside of nocturnal dream states and viewed as 'a regressive capacity for thinking akin to the form of a primitive state of the psychical – apparatus in which wishing ended in hallucinating' (Freud, 1900, p. 566) of which 'the night dream is a relic'. For the Botellas, the hallucination occurs as accident or absence (in thinking), and for Bion and those who follow him, reverie also has a similar 'unbidden' quality. Furthermore, both Bion and the Botellas place emphasis on the analyst's regressive experience during the session and where Bion may have emphasized the importance of linking, the Botellas emphasize the *analyst's* ability to 'create new connections, new contents' through his application of the figurability of thought as a reflection of and complement to the analysand's regressive psychic functioning that can 'give access to unrepresentable areas of the analysand's mind that would otherwise remain unreachable' (p. 83). This is what, following Green's suggestion that the analyst lend themselves to the fusional needs of the patient, they refer to as the analyst working as a 'double' to the patient.

A third variation

A more thorough conceptualization of dreaming in the analytic pair is supplied by Bollas (1995) who reads Freud's metaphor of an unconscious receiver as processing 'the patient's unconscious communications on its own terms: one dreamer to another' (p. 12). Bollas describes how he allies his state of mind with the patient's unconscious by adopting a mentality that is timeless, plastic and open to contradiction, and thus meets the unconscious sensibility of the patient. The patient, sensing this receptivity on the part of the analyst, puts both himself and his objects into the analyst's dreaming, contributing to it and using the analyst as a participant in his own increased unconsciousness. Here we might say that in positioning himself as receiver of the patient's unconscious communication, Bollas does not only passively receive these messages. Through engaging in a process of deep associative listening, both to the patient and to himself, he finds those objects the patient has unconsciously entrusted to the inner world of the analyst and allows himself to 'drop into' them and be guided by his own countertransferential dreaming inhabits them. Thus in dreaming with the analysand during the hour, Bollas describes being transported to another place, transformed into another person or experiencing events and places as changed.

Bollas (1995) writes,

> The analyst listening to the patient's chain of ideas in that special frame of mind that is characterized by evenly hovering attentiveness . . . as Freud implies . . . free-associates to his patient, drifting *away* through associative pathways of his own, riding the patient's narrative, sometimes like a child following a storytelling parent, or a scientist stopping to ponder a thing or two before catching up again. An idea, an image, a word falls out of the blue – what Freud termed *Einfall* (a mental content that simply drops in uninvited by consciousness) – and often these are riotously anticontextual. This complex psychic movement – a kind of *countertransference dreaming* – reflects the analyst's consistent topographical response as he transforms the patient's material according to the laws of the dream work: displacing the patient's narrative into a counternarrative, condensing the patient's descriptions with this patient's other accounts, incorporating the analysand's mood into his own emotional constellation, altering an image or changing a word, bearing the analysand's psychic state within his own body thus creating his own somatic double to the patient.
>
> (p. 12)

Bollas follows Freud's attempt to catch the drift of the patient's unconscious with his own unconscious. He does so through listening to the patient, confident in the fact that he does not know what he is listening to or for. Bollas describes his analytic listening in this manner as similar in some respects to the dream work before the dream scene, wherein an unconscious area of work gives the analytic pair a sense of its presence. He writes,

It is difficult to describe how I listen to the analysand within the session. The endless slide of words, signifiers that evoke limitless associations just as they suggest specific links that imply precise meaning, the images that bring me to a formed world in that strange intimacy of co-imagining. Often patients indicate through diction texture, hesitation, body state, and expectation those moments in a session that are of particular significance . . . Yet in the midst of all that I usually feel that this patient and I are at work on something. Something beyond our consciousness yet unconsciously compelling. Something that seems to draw us to it, so that ideas, interpretations, and associations that feel off center of this inner pull are discarded. Something we know but as yet cannot think. Some interpretations, views, questions, feel more in touch with that unthought known area being worked on, even though they seem no more plausible than the abandoned ideas.

(pp. 76–77)

Where the wild things are

Examining the way Bion, Ogden, the Botellas or Bollas work, by dreaming and hallucinating with the patient, may lead one to the quick impression that these are wild and undisciplined approaches, free from considerations of technique. Yet I have shown how they are grounded in Freudian and post-Freudian conceptualizations of unconscious communication. While excellent critiques of other analytic schools that eschew a theory of technique exist (e.g. Tublin, 2011), the approaches described here are thought-through systems of abnegation by the analyst, silence and willingness to be affected. In each, the analyst enters a disciplined precondition for the creation of an analytic space that will facilitate experiences of unconscious contact, and while these analysts travel to 'where the wild things are', to quote the title of Maurice Sendak's (1963) famous children's book, their technique is anything but wild. It involves putting aside memory and desire as well as understanding and preconception so that the analyst can 'become' the object. But this becoming is not a fusion, according to Grotstein (2004), who wrote that in processing the hidden emotional truths of the patient, the analyst 'is evoked, provoked or 'primed' (Helm, unpublished) to respond to the analysand's emotions and association with his or her own private, native emotions that are independently summoned within him or her – that the analyst's alpha function, working in a state of reverie, allows the analyst to enter within his or her own unconscious to locate and summon (unconsciously) those emotions and experiences that are apposite to the hidden emotional truths of the analysand with which they symmetrically resonate, thereby achieving a 'common sense' (Bion, 1963, p. 10) corroboration of the analysand's emotions, and furthermore establishing the 'clinical truth' of the moment'. These areas of emotional experiencing are often saturated with pain as noted earlier by Ogden, and the truths revealed laden with risk, making their pursuit, in de M'Uzan's words, 'a policy at the edge of the abyss'.

These experiences are the everyday currency of analysis, and while their more dramatic forms are the ones most often reported in the literature, the quotidian aspects of unconscious intersubjective engagement are always present and operative. A simple example from my own practice will illustrate this. I chose this example for two reasons: first, it's a brief illustration rather than an extended reverie that nevertheless makes the point about the patient's dreaming alongside the analyst and the analyst's associations. Secondly, it is an example that I think illustrates how much work of the analysis happens outside of interpretative exchange, i.e. within the unconscious intersubjective relation itself.

In listening to Mrs. C's complaint that her husband did not 'take care of her' as she wished, I associated to the potential sexual meanings, to her early history as an infant and later as a child who was passed on by her mother to a series of African-American nannies to whom Mrs. C had become attached and then lost in succession, and to themes within the transference-countertransference. However, after hearing these words for an extended time I began to feel bothered by them, feeling they were not the right words to describe what she was attempting to say. I did not know what the right words were, but this feeling stayed with me over several weeks while the patient continued her narrative.

In one session, following the recent death of Aretha Franklin, the image of pink Cadillacs assembled at the singer's funeral entered my mind, seemingly unrelated to what Mrs. C was saying. Very quickly afterwards, I heard the word R E S P E C T spelled out in my mind, as in the song. Involuntarily, I smiled at the message and felt it to be reflective of the sort of anticontextual countertransference dreaming described by Bollas. I did not fashion an interpretation from the experience, merely sat with this new perspective. Two sessions later, Mrs. C declared that what she wanted from her husband was for him to respect her, that she felt the things he didn't do for her were signs of his disrespect towards her.

The dream image represents a condensation of all of the factors I had consciously considered in my associations – the sexual content conveyed by Ms. Franklin's metaphor of the pink Cadillac, which in the song 'Freeway of Love' represents the vagina and sexual pleasure. Ms. Franklin's race and gender surely were pieces of the condensation that linked her in my mind to the patient's experience of being brought up by African-American nannies, but the particular association to her funeral I believe in retrospect was linked to the overwhelming expression of love for this woman who touched so many people and brought so much joy and was lost. Thus themes of dependence, erotization, love, gratitude and loss all were condensed in this image and related to the unconscious maternal erotic transference and my 'care' of the patient. The leap to the word 'respect' also came associatively, bringing with it an additional area of the patient's unconscious experiencing not included in my conscious associations while listening to Mrs. C, though present in liminal form in the feeling I had been experiencing regarding her use of particular words to describe her complaint relating to her husband.

We can see in the three approaches surveyed in this chapter how Freud's writings on accessing unconscious processes are utilized by these authors in their notions of entering dreamlike states, spaces of regression in parallel with their patients, which help them find something mysterious, something perhaps alien. Each of the authors discussed is engaged in trying to develop meaning from an experience they have in themselves – that is to say, from having allowed themselves to have been affected, shaped and contacted by their patient's unconscious. They do this to reach depths of psychic life that are undreamt and thus unlived. They do this to make 'figurable' previously unrepresented experience. And they do this to expand the patient's range of unconscious engagement and their ability to think. Each of these authors reclaims Freud's writing on dreaming and hallucination, and repurposes it to Thoreau's vision of our truest life – 'in dreams awake'.

References

Bion, W. R. (1963). *Elements of Psycho-Analysis*. London: Heinemann.
Bollas, C. (1995). *Cracking Up: The Work of Unconscious Experience*. New York: Hill & Wang.
Botella, S. & Botella, C. (2005). *The Work of Psychic Figurability: Mental States Without Representation*. New York: Routledge.
Britton, R. & Steiner, J. (1994). 'Interpretation: Selected Fact or Overvalued Idea?' *International Journal of Psychoanalysis*, 75: 1069–1078.
Brown, L. (2011). *Intersubjective Processes and the Unconscious*. New York: Routledge.
De M'Uzan, M. (2003). 'Slaves of Quantity.' *Psychoanalytic Quarterly*, 72: 711–725.
Falcão, L. (2017). 'The Hallucinatory in the Analytic Session.' Presented at IPA, Buenos Aires.
Ferro, A. (2009). 'Transformations in Dreaming and Characters in the Psychoanalytic Field.' *International Journal of Psychoanalysis*, 90: 209–230.
Ferro, A. (2017). *Contemporary Bionian Theory and Technique in Psychoanalysis*. New York: Routledge.
Fonagy, P., Gergely, G., Jurist, E. & Target, M. (2004). *Affect Regulation, Mentalization, and the Development of the Self*. New York: Other Press.
Freud, S. (1900). *The Interpretation of Dreams*. SEV, London: Hogarth Press, pp. 339–685.
Freud, S. (1912). 'Recommendations to Physicians Practicing Psycho-Analysis.' *S.E.*, Vol. XII, London: Hogarth Press, pp. 109–120.
Freud, S. (1913). 'On Beginning the Treatment.' *S.E.*, Vol. XII, London: Hogarth Press, pp. 121–144.
Freud, S. (1915). 'The Unconscious.' *S.E.*, Vol. XIV, London: Hogarth Press, pp. 159–215.
Freud, S. (1922). 'Dreams and Telepathy.' *S.E.*, Vol. XVIII, London: Hogarth Press, pp. 195–220.
Green, A. (1975). 'The Analyst, Symbolization and Absence in the Analytic Setting (On Changes in Analytic Practice and Analytic Experience) – In Memory of D. W. Winnicott.' *International Journal of Psycho-Analysis*, 56: 1–22.
Green, A. (1998). 'The Primordial Mind and the Work of the Negative.' *International Journal of Psycho-Analysis*, 79: 649–665.
Grotstein, J.S. (2004). '"The Light Militia of the Lower Sky": The Deeper Nature of Dreaming and Phantasying.' *Psychoanalytic Dialogues*, 14(1): 99–118.

Grotstein, J. (1997). 'Bion's "Transformation in 'O'" and the Concept of the "Transcendent Position."' www.sicap.it/merciai/bion/papers/grots.htm. [Google Scholar].

McDougall, J. (1984). 'The "Dis-affected" Patient: Reflections on Affect Pathology.' *Psychoanalytic Quarterly*, 53: 386–409.

Ogden, T.H. (1994). 'The Analytic Third: Working with Intersubjective Clinical Facts.' *International Journal of Psychoanalysis*, 75: 3–19.

Ogden, T.H. (2005). 'On Not Being Able to Dream.' In: *This Art of Psychoanalysis: Dreaming Undreamt Dreams and Interrupted Cries*. New York: Routledge, pp. 45–60.

Ogden, T.H. (2007). 'On Talking-as-Dreaming.' *International Journal of Psychoanalysis*, 88: 575–589.

Perelberg, R.J. (2016). 'Negative Hallucinations, Dreams and Hallucinations: The Framing Structure and Its Representation in the Analytic Setting.' *International Journal of Psychoanalysis*, 97: 1575–1590.

Reed, G. (2015). 'Andre Green on the Theory and Treatment of "Non-Neurotic" Patients.' *Psychoanalytic Review*, 102(5): 649–658.

Sendak, M. (1963). *Where the Wild Things Are*. New York: Harper & Row.

Schneider, J.A. (2010). 'From Freud's Dream-Work to Bion's Work of Dreaming: The Changing Conception of Dreaming in Psychoanalytic Theory.' *International Journal of Psycho-Analysis*, 91(3): 521–540.

Thoreau, H.D. (1980). *A Week on the Concord and Merrimack Rivers*. Carl F. Hove, William L. Howarth & Elizabeth Hall Witherell (Eds.). Princeton, NJ: Princeton University Press.

Tublin, S. (2011). 'Discipline and Freedom in Relational Technique.' *Contemporary Psychoanalysis*, 47(4): 519–546.

Tustin, F. (1981). *Autistic States in Children*. Boston, MA: Routledge & Kegan Paul, 276 p.

Wilson, M. (2018). 'The Analyst as Listening-Accompanist: Desire in Bion and Lacan.' *Psychoanalytic Quarterly*, 87(2): 237–264. DOI: 10.1080/00332828.2018.1450597.

Winnicott, D.W. (1958). 'Primary Maternal Preoccupation.' In: *Collected Papers: Through Paediatrics to Psycho-Analysis*. London: Tavistock Publications; New York: Basic Books, 1956, pp. 300–305.

Chapter 3

Zombie states
Reconsidering the relationship between life and death instincts

Where the dialectical relation between the life and death instincts becomes dissociated, what we might call 'zombie states' result, in which individuals inhabit deadness as if it were aliveness. Bypassing reservations on the speculative nature of these instincts, I would like to highlight certain clinical phenomena that might be lost to current ways of conceptualizing aliveness and deadness. I will revisit what has been written about psychic deadness to argue that these states actually reflect an alive deadness, a zombie-like condition, where the individual is neither depressively collapsed (dead) nor fully alive, but animated in his deadness without self-reflective capacities or idiomatic signatures. The experience is of a pull towards non-human states, not being a person or of being an inanimate object. I will use a clinical vignette to illustrate particular countertransference difficulties associated with aliveness and deadness in the analytic situation, as well as the powerful contagion associated with what I term zombie states.

Speculative, even for Freud, the actual existence of the death instinct may be less important than its heuristic value to us in working clinically with those individuals who do not appear to be fully alive or fully dead. But my aim here is to leverage the idea of a death instinct to allow for a reconsideration of clinical phenomena that may, otherwise, be lost by relegating this concept to non-existence. I would like to discuss the death instinct as a way of thinking about a motive force towards nothingness and dedifferentiation which has been described by several authors.

Within psychoanalytic literature, one will find descriptions of patients who are psychically dead, who experience non-human states, and relate to themselves and others as if they are objects rather than human beings. Such individuals may resemble fully human, fully alive persons, but on closer examination lack an experience not only of self-awareness but also subjectivity. These persons appear to have no idiomatic signature, no trace of human uniqueness or distinctiveness. Often the term psychic deadness is used to describe an emotional flatness or depressive psychic mien, and the individuals described in this chapter may well experience such affective disturbances, but their experience of deadness extends to more than just the affective sphere. They are not depressively collapsed, depersonalized following a trauma or simply schizoid; they are animated in their deadness – i.e. they are living a deadness that they have come to inhabit as if it were a full experience of aliveness.

I propose to reconsider states of deadness by situating the death instinct in dialectical relation to the life instincts. Conceiving of the relation of these forces in this way may allow the clinician to regard his patient as neither simply alive nor dead, but central to an investigation of this kind is a reaffirmation of the existence and power of the death drive, a much contested, though still very clinically relevant part of contemporary psychoanalytic practice (Kernberg, 2009). Whereas in a stimulus-response model of mental functioning, depersonalization is understood as a dissociative response to external trauma; I will suggest that in a psychoanalytic model, the dissociation that occurs in zombie states is a dissociation of the relationship of dialectical interpenetration between life and death instincts.

The death instinct may be seen to have two sides, or meanings: one associated with hatred/aggression and the other with a pull towards nothingness/dedifferentiation. Here I would like to examine the latter meaning and thus will not be describing the more blatantly sadistic, aggressive or self-destructive individuals one might more commonly identify with manifestations of the death instinct, but persons who experience an intense draw towards sameness, and a lack of a sense of interiority. After surveying several authors' descriptions of such persons, I will move to a discussion of the Freudian death instinct and then to a description of zombie states.

My intent in analogizing these persons mental states to the fictional character of the zombie is in no way to make light of very serious deficits but rather to provide a different understanding of the experience of a group of people who inhabit life without subjective involvement. It will be beyond the scope of this chapter to consider the aetiology of these states, and I will not presume to make claims as to how zombie states arise. I will, however, illustrate through a clinical vignette that approaching the issue of aliveness and deadness from this different perspective may help the analyst avoid a form of dichotomous thinking and certain countertransference difficulties that may follow from such thinking.

Missing persons: non-human states in characterological disorders

One of Winnicott's most important contributions to psychoanalysis was his questioning of the classical assumption that the patient was already a person. Greenberg and Mitchell (1983) observed that Winnicott remedied our having overlooked patients who 'only *appear* to interact with others' (p. 191). In identifying the 'as-if' personality Deutsch (1942) described such individuals, who give an initial impression of 'complete normality' (p. 303) but who lack both emotional depth and any indication of individuality. In encountering these patients one has, Deutsch wrote, 'the inescapable impression that the individual's whole relationship to life has something about it which is lacking in genuineness and yet outwardly runs along 'as if' it were complete' (p. 303). These people may be intellectually intact, but their work is totally devoid of originality. Rather than reflecting a creative impulse, 'it is always a laborious though skillful imitation of a model without the slightest personal trace' (Deutsch, 1942). The absence of a personal presence is central to Deutsch's understanding of the inner emptiness of these individuals whose impoverished emotional experience hides a lack of human feeling and personal inclination behind a superficial adaptation: 'Outwardly he conducts his life as if he possessed a complete and sensitive emotional capacity. To him there is no difference between his empty forms and what others actually experience' (p. 304). If given an example to follow, these people enthusiastically blend in to social, ethical or religious groups, instrumentally adopting their practices, but ready to change them at a moment's notice should the need arise. They are

> completely without character, wholly unprincipled, in the literal sense of the term, the morals of the 'as-if' individuals, their ideals, their convictions are simply reflections of another person, good or bad [they do this] to give content and reality to their inner emptiness and establish the validity of their existence by identification.
>
> (p. 304)

Due to their detachment and unresponsiveness, Deutsch considered them to be 'de-personalized'.

A similar presentation is described by Bollas (1987) in the 'normotic character', who is more intrinsically related than the as-if character, yet at the same time disinclined 'to entertain the subjective element in life, whether it exists inside himself or in the other' (p. 137). Instead, normotic individuals attempt to erase what traces of subjective life they have in favour of becoming a non-human object. According to Bollas (1987), their quest is to be so 'normal' as to erase any creative trace of idiosyncratic individuality (p. 152).

McDougall (1982) has described clinical encounters with 'normopaths'. Like Bollas's normotics, they are people who attempt to eradicate the self from subjective life, killing imagination and choosing psychic death over creativity (Kohon, 1999). In treatment, they make for 'anti-analysands' (McDougall, 1978) able to quickly and superficially adapt to the analytic situation but not the analytic process. McDougall (1978) writes that these individuals are under the spell of a force that exerts 'a massive strength that is only revealed through its negative effect' (p. 215) on thinking, dreaming, relatedness and creativity. Their impoverished inner processes are linked by McDougall to the operation of an 'anti-life force' (p. 233).

This force is similarly described by Green (1999) as producing a 'disobjectualising function' which wipes out memory, mind, contact with other people and the feeling of being alive (p. 220). The individual undergoing these effects does not experience a sense of lack or absence but instead uses the feeling of lack or absence as 'the substratum for what is real' (p. 209). As a consequence, the object world loses its specificity and qualities of individuality, and an inclination sets in towards 'self-disappearance' (p. 220).

Non-human states in psychotic conditions

It bears mentioning that non-human states have also been described in psychotic individuals. Searles (1960) has written of the impulse to dedifferentiate one's self from other humans and rejoin the life of the non-human environment from which he understands the individual to have emerged. As a defence against various feeling states the non-human realm represents an escape from the problems of living. Searles (1960) writes,

> At times when our lives as human beings seem intolerably filled with complex decisions to be resolved, and with complex feelings to be borne within ourselves, we may wish that we could put all this aside by achieving what may appear to us to be the enviably passive, simple existence of various non-human forms of life, or even of inanimate objects.
>
> (p. 226)

He links such a desire to the death instinct suggesting that one's biological fate, to return to a non-human state, holds deep psychological significance in the psychic life of the living individual.

Ogden (1980, 1982) also has written of states of 'non-experience' in schizophrenic individuals wherein the person lives partly in a state of psychological deadness – 'that is, there are sectors of his personality in which even unconscious meanings and affects cease to be elaborated' (Ogden, 1989).

Forms of aliveness and deadness

While not describing precisely the same phenomena, each of the previous clinical descriptions broadly depicts experiences of not being human. Such states may be manifested as deadness, as a feeling that one is akin to a physical object or the natural environment, or as not being a person. The experience of such states may vary from the transient, such as in the use of a defence as Searles described, to the characterological, in the way that Deutsch and others have described. The psychoanalytic literature has traditionally associated such states with psychotic individuals and the more characterologically disturbed, but recently it has been suggested that forms of deadness may represent a more pervasive impediment to the experience of feeling alive across a spectrum of human difficulties. Ogden (1997) for one has commented, 'I believe that every form of psychopathology represents a specific type of limitation of the individual's capacity to be fully alive as a human being' (p. 26). Since there exists a range as well as a profusion of non-human experiencing, it may be useful to revisit the ways in which analysts have discussed issues of aliveness and deadness, and the clinical approaches that have followed from these conceptualizations.

For the most part, analysts have tended to treat aliveness and deadness as dichotomous, all or nothing terms. It is often discussed as a goal that a patient will feel 'fully alive', and we speak of 'psychic deadness' as if these experiences necessarily preclude each other as they would biologically. Even where these states are partial, they tend to be described in all or nothing terms, such as 'areas of psychic deadness' where the remainder of the personality is understood to be alive. Further, it is assumed that a diminishment in one experience will necessarily lead to an increase in the other. As may be expected from this bifurcation, areas of deadness are supposed to shrink through analysis, allowing an individual to become more subjectively present, more alive, more fully human (e.g. Shoshani, 2009). Inherent in the dichotomization of these terms is the assumption that life is good and death bad (Abel-Hirsch, 2010). But to conceive of matters in this way is to run the risk of oversimplifying the relation these instincts have to each other. Instead of regarding states of aliveness and deadness as exclusive of each other we may instead regard them as dialectically constituting each other, as Freud (1937, p. 243) described, 'Only by the concurrent of mutually opposing action of the two primal instincts – Eros and the death instinct – never by one or the other alone, can we explain the rich multiplicity of the phenomena of life'. Thus we move psychically from deadness to living and back again in the manner of Bion's double arrows (1970). Deadness and aliveness infuse each other in normal functioning, and it is the dissociation of this relation that results in psychopathological conditions of non-human states.

The relation of life and death instincts

Freud's concept of the death instinct was posited as a force that impels humans to strive for a return to the non-organic (i.e. non-living, non-human) state from which they first arose. In 'Beyond the Pleasure Principle' (1920), Freud suggested this instinct 'arise[s] from the coming to life of inanimate matter and seek[s] to restore the inanimate state' (p. 44). Yet the death instinct exists alongside the life instinct, which promotes survival, pleasure and reproduction. These forces are counterbalanced, creating a relationship of opposition. In 'Civilisation and Its Discontents' (1930), Freud explained,

> Starting from speculations on the beginning of life and from biological parallels, I drew the conclusion that, besides the instinct to preserve living substance and to join it into ever larger units, there must exist another, contrary instinct seeking to dissolve those units and to bring them back to their primeval, inorganic state. That is to say, as well as Eros there was an instinct of death. The phenomena of life could be explained from the *concurrent or mutually opposing action of these two instincts*.
>
> (pp. 118–119, my italics)

Freud (1920) observed how the normal interplay of these instincts was crucial in their healthy modification, describing, for instance, the role the libido plays in directing the death instinct outwards. He also observed how various disturbances result from the imbalance of these forces, such as the condition of moral masochism, thought to result from the portion of the death instinct 'which has escaped being turned outwards as an instinct of destruction' (1924, p. 170) and the condition of melancholia that represents 'a pure culture of the death instinct' (1923, p. 53) when the superego is wholly governed by this force. The opposition Freud proposed between these instinctual forces is crucial to the constitution of experience, and the essential tension created by this opposition represents the infusion of the death instinct in alive experiencing. Rather than viewing the relationship between these instincts as one of fusion, as Freud did, I would like to suggest their relationship is one of dialectical, mutual creation. Ogden (1994) described it thusly,

> Dialectic is a process in which opposing elements each create, preserve, and negate the other; each stands in a dynamic, ever-changing relationship to the other. Dialectical movement tends toward integrations that are never achieved. Each potential integration creates a new form of opposition characterized by its own distinct form of dialectical tension. That which is generated dialectically is continuously in motion, perpetually in the process of being created and negated, perpetually in the process of being decentered from static self-evidence.
>
> (p. 14)

In applying a dialectic view to the life and death instincts, we might say that in order to truly appreciate life, one must implicitly accept death. Only then can experiencing become poignant or precious, precisely because of the balance and interpenetration of instinctual forces. As a dialectical process, life and death instincts create an opposition that allows for a dialectical tension – i.e. a sense of the movement of creation and negation in one's experience. Freud wrote of the imbalance of life and death instincts, and what happens when one opposing force dominates the other and blocks this movement. Placing instinctual forces in opposition resulted in an explanation for 'the phenomena of life', which I take to mean psychic life as well as biological life. I would like to investigate what occurs when there is a *collapse* of tension between these forces. It is my contention that such a collapse results in a state of living deadness. Segal (1997) wrote of the pull towards nothingness/dedifferentiation 'the need to annihilate the perceiving experiencing self, as well as anything that is perceived' (p. 18). From my perspective, such de-personalization does not represent the problematic introduction of dissociative defences but signals the loss of an essential dialectic between life and death instinct. Relational writers such as Bromberg (2011), who favour a dissociative model of the mind, write of depersonalization resulting from the affective dysregulation that accompanies the experience of external trauma. In my view, not all depersonalization is necessarily trauma related. Here I am concerned with the subject's instinctual life in the absence of identifiable traumatic antecedents, and so I have refrained from using the term dissociation in order to spare the reader the presumption of an all too familiar aetiology. Indeed, the case illustration that follows is meant to question the predominance of traumatic aetiology as an explanatory in the absence of clinical evidence that would support that claim.

Zombie states

The cultural trope of the zombie captures the experience of non-human or depersonalized states in a manner different from an individual's aliveness or deadness. In the popular imagination, zombies are neither fully alive nor are they simply dead. They inhabit a condition of living deadness, existing as mindless yet animated human forms without complex purpose or basic subjectivity. For our discussion, it is important to note that zombies hunger for and feed on the brains of other (non-zombie) humans. Not incidentally, their contact with humans represents a powerful opportunity for contagion. Such contagion is often represented in film by the incidental exchange of fluids which transform the non-zombie human into a mindless automaton. So spreads the plague of absent agency that reflects the dullness of non-conscious beings.

Within philosophy of mind Chalmers (1996) has utilized the concept of the philosophical zombie to argue against materialist and behaviouralist conceptions of human beings. Chalmers imagines a person who is physically indistinguishable from a regular living person, who acts perfectly normal but who is not conscious. Lacking sentience, these individuals appear very much like the as-if or normotic personalities described in our literature. For our purposes as psychoanalysts, we might say that Chalmers's argument is aimed at reinforcing the centrality of interiority to human existence. It is a welcomed argument for psychoanalysts living in a so-called post-human world, which has created a rent between traditional notions of identity and humanness (Haraway, 1990).

Lacking experience of subjective interiority, individuals in zombie states often belong to and follow groups without personal conviction or an actual sense of purpose. They may *appear* to interact with others, but, in fact, be without a self that would facilitate mutual exchange between people. Thus they exhibit little or no interest in others as others and have difficulty in understanding other's interest in them. The philosopher Baudrillard (2000) understood this dimension of zombie psychic states when he wrote,

> The death drive, according to Freud, is precisely this nostalgia for a state before the appearance of individuality and sexual differentiation, a state in which we lived before we became mortal and distinct from one another. Absolute death is not the end of the individual human being; rather, it is a regression toward a state of minimal differentiation among living beings, of a pure repetition of identical beings.
>
> (p. 6)

Analytic engagement

Clinical interactions with these people can seem lifeless, stale, suffocating and threatening to the analyst's subjective experiencing. Ogden describes this dimension of the work when writing about experiences in the transference-countertransference in which he reports feeling he was losing the use of his mind. Reflecting on his experience in sessions with such a patient, Ogden (1997) wrote,

> I began to be able to link the experience of holding my own wrist (in the act of taking my pulse) with what I now suspected to be a need to literally feel human warmth in an effort to reassure myself that I was alive and healthy. This realization brought with it a profound shift in my understanding of a great many aspects of my experience with Ms. N. I felt moved by the patient's tenacity in telling me seemingly pointless stories for more than 18 months. It occurred to me that these stories had been offered with the unconscious hope that I might find (or create) a point to the stories thereby creating a point (a feeling of coherence, direction, value, and authenticity) for the patient's life. I had previously been conscious of my own fantasy of feigning illness in order to escape the stagnant deadness of the sessions, but I had not understood that this 'excuse' reflected an unconscious fantasy that I was being made ill by prolonged exposure to the lifelessness of the analysis.
> (p. 31)

Bion (1959) and others have noted the attacks on linking, the efforts to destroy the inner mental processes of the analyst. What Ogden describes as the fear that he was losing the use of his own mind and his feeling the need to reassure himself that he was human, alive and living in a world of meaning may well reflect the type of phenomena I am proposing is metaphorically associated with popular depictions of zombies eating the brains of others.[1] Clearly, a powerful contagion exists in encountering these states clinically and the analyst may often have to struggle to regain a feeling of humanness.

Vignette

During the initial consultation, Michael told me that more than one woman he had dated and taken home to his Manhattan apartment had nervously joked that maybe he was a serial killer. It turned out these women had intuited more than they could consciously know about Michael. Their jokes reflected an experience of him that I would soon be privy to as well. His modern apartment had nothing on the walls, no books in the bookcases and no personal items or mementos on display. As Michael revealed more of himself, it became clear that he didn't watch television or go to the cinema. He had no hobbies and no strong preferences for music or food. Raised in the Christian faith, Michael had no relationship to his religion, and deferred any investigation both of metaphysical and practical matters, such as whether he believed in the existence of a God, or in the observation of meaningful ritual, all the while maintaining that he was 'Catholic'. It wasn't so much that Michael didn't understand my inquires about his religious or his political beliefs, instead he expressed that he had absolutely no interest in ever thinking about these matters, either with me or on his own.

In addition to coming to his analysis multiple times weekly, Michael also saw a personal trainer several times a week. It wasn't that he enjoyed the exercise itself or relished physical challenges, but Michael felt having 'a good body' would be attractive to women he might meet. Sexual desire itself, however, was problematic. He collected experiences with women much like someone would collect objects he knew were valuable, but that actually had no aesthetic appeal to him. Highly successful in his field, Michael spent his time shuttling around the country, deciding whether to spend extra days at five-star luxury hotels or extend his weekends in foreign cities. Deciding was particularly hard for Michael as he seemed to have no personal preferences. Instead, he would often consult me on what I thought the 'right' choice would be regarding what to have for dinner, or where to spend his vacation time. Should he buy an expensive bicycle, should he rent a house in a beach community for the summer? Michael had no way to decide, other than to see what others did with their time and attempt to do the same.

He had undertaken an analysis in order to treat a depression diagnosed and medicated by his physician, but after weaning himself off of his antidepressants, it became clear he hadn't been clinically depressed, and what the physician had taken to be a mood disorder were signs of Michael's inner deadness. The force that had seemingly annihilated Michael's self soon took residence in the transference-countertransference.[2] From early on in our meetings, I experienced a profound hollowness when listening to Michael, one that often left me feeling lonely, as if I were the only one in the room. There was never a sense of connection, or mutuality or even the type of wordless familiarity that analyst and patient often share after extended periods of intimate, intense exchange.

Over time, I began to feel as if I'd been worked on, as if my patient's emptiness had taken a cumulative toll on me, leaving me feeling not just alone in the analysis, but weary and mentally dull. No dreams or fantasies were ever reported. Michael exhibited no curiosity about his mind or mine. Events for him occurred on a level of concreteness that profoundly precluded reflection or thought on his part and increasingly on my own. Interpretations landed nowhere and were met with what can only be called an absence of cognition. However, I am quite sure that I didn't go down without a fight, and in retrospect, I can understand a period of my increasing engagement with Michael as an unconscious attempt to counteract creeping feelings of suffocation in the countertransference. Of note was one interpretation that I felt to be uncharacteristically harsh, where I suggested to Michael that his difficulties in making decisions and knowing what it was he liked resulted from him missing a self that might feel more strongly about one thing over another. But Michael was neither interested nor taken aback by the interpretation. Rather than express curiosity at what I may have meant, he simply disagreed, though he couldn't say *why* he felt he was a self.

While I constantly questioned myself as to whether I was having any effect on Michael, he clearly was having an effect on me. It is inconceivable to me that anyone would not have been able to recognize my gradual decline into analytic stagnation, yet Michael gave no indication that he was aware of having any impact on me at all. Was this what somehow had to happen in the analysis? Was this a recreation of an early object relation? Was my countertransference state something Michael had to sense unconsciously as happening within me – but what, if anything, could he sense? I couldn't tell if we were suffering something together, and anxiously, I wondered whether the treatment itself would *survive*. This was a relationship marked by a ghostly absence, one that I tried in vain to fill with understanding of his condition and its aetiology. In retrospect, I believe these attempts at thinking with my patient were my attempts to stay alive by making sense of or by believing that there was some hidden true self-expression I didn't see, that there may have been an early trauma that itself had been sucked into a black hole and that the flatness he conveyed was surely a surface phenomenon under which there must lie substance and humanity, an individual, a soul.

It was subsequent to this period in the analysis, though I wasn't aware of it, that my interactions with Michael took on a pro forma quality. I was already engaged in the production of a facsimile of an analysis, and my comments and questions to him were under the sway of a force much greater than mere boredom or defeat.

By the third year of analysis, I experienced frequent feelings of being adrift, as if in the ocean, on a raft, by myself. No longer fighting the 'worked over' feeling, I simply allowed myself to listen. Michael regularly attended his sessions, spoke about work and his difficulties making decisions, and I rose and fell with the swells of his monologue. Eventually, a reverie set in, during which I repeatedly saw in my mind images of the kind usually found in supermarket tabloids, where celebrities and their 'lifestyles' are portrayed in glamorous colour photographs. As I became aware of these images, I also became aware of my enjoyment of the attractiveness these photos portrayed and the depiction of the carefree pursuit of pleasure in faraway places. For sure it was one way off my raft, but there was more to it than just that. When I considered the images, I found them to be free of anxiety – in fact, they displayed the very opposite of anxiety. They were pictures of an easy, fully indulged life without conflict. There was no boredom, no existential condition to have to contend with, no pain or mundane entanglements such as illness or financial concerns. In this world, there were no difficulties, no missed airplanes or phones that stopped working, and if there were, they were problems that could quickly be fixed and moved on from. And it didn't matter whether it was an airplane or a human relationship, a cell phone or another person, the point was that any trouble or even the potential to become ensnared in regular human existence was just absent.

I started to consider how these glossy images might have signalled my own unconscious fantasy to live a non-human life, a zombie life. And I understood that in my efforts to try to bring Michael back to life, I had occluded my envy of the ease of his living deadness. The only word I can think to describe the feeling that emerged is that Michael's 'life' had a certain *seductiveness* to it, which seemed to promise escape from the difficulties associated with the human condition. Here was the seductiveness of the death drive, the siren call to extinguish my own idiomatic presence and follow Michael's path towards the 'zero point' (Laplanche & Pontalis, 1973, p. 97). This realization, if it may be called that, was enough to wake me from my stupor. My ability to have this thought at all is similar to what Symington (1983) described as the analyst's inner act of freedom. The experience felt like coming up for air, and I filled my lungs, in the process coming back to a mental presence in which I could appreciate Michael's externally attractive and psychologically void lifestyle. Eventually, I said to Michael that while I felt he lived an exciting and even enviable life, it seemed to me that no matter how glossy and shiny he tried to make it, all the hotels, beach houses and beautiful women ultimately failed to satisfy a need inside him, and that living his life in this way was missing the point of having a life.

This comment followed the lines of Winnicott's (1965a) guidance in attempting to communicate with the patient's True Self. He wrote,

> A principle might be enunciated, that in the False Self area of our analytic practice we find we make more headway by recognition of the patient's non-existence than by a long-continued working with the patient on the basis of ego-defence mechanisms. The patient's False Self can collaborate indefinitely with the analyst in the analysis of defences, being so to speak on the analyst's side in the game. This unrewarding work is only cut short profitably when the analyst can point to and specify an absence of some essential feature: 'you have no mouth', 'You have not started to exist yet', 'physically you are a man, but you do not know from experience anything about masculinity', and so on. These recognitions of important fact, made clear at the right moments, pave the way for communication with the True Self.
>
> (p. 142)

Michael responded associatively by telling me a story about a woman he had brought to his apartment the week before. Having very recently redone the wood floors (glossy, shiny) in his apartment and insisting that the flooring company come back three times to redo the surface because the job was not quite perfect and he could detect subtle flaws, Michael invited Amy to his place after their dinner. Because he wasn't paying attention, he didn't notice that Amy's high-heeled shoes created tiny indentations in the soft wood on his new floor. When he discovered this the next day, he was terribly upset. But then he considered that he would like to see Amy again and that he could, if he really wanted, have the floors redone at his own expense. In fact, he was thinking of moving to a larger apartment so perhaps it made sense to tolerate the small indentations in the floor until he moved to another place. What was striking about this story was that Michael came up with this solution on his own, without asking me what I felt he should do. He felt that he liked Amy enough to live with slightly marred floors. She liked going to the gym as he did, and as they spent more time together, he took on her interests, beginning to watch the television shows she liked and planning vacations with her.

The fact that Michael and Amy came from different religious backgrounds caused some consternation for both their families. Yet Michael decided on his own that he would endure the comments of his family in order to spend his time with Amy. He did, in fact, complain bitterly to me about the look of the floors in his apartment, but he held that feeling, and when he did after a time move from there it was with Amy, whom Michael now told me he loved, though I never detected an expression of affection in his voice.

Michael's life continued to improve over the course of the next several years of the treatment. He married, had a daughter, moved to a home in the suburbs; ultimately though, he remained who he had always been. For instance, he had no preference regarding moving to the suburbs, but several of the couple's friends had begun to do so as they started families. Michael then thought that this is what he and his family should do, and he asked me what I thought he should do. I said to Michael that a move like this would represent a major change in his life with Amy and a new chapter for their family. He agreed, and several months later, the couple closed on a home in a somewhat distant community. In moving, Michael discontinued his treatment, thanking me for everything, saying that he never could have done all he had over the course of our work together if it weren't for me. After years of analytic treatment, I had the feeling that I'd never actually met Michael and that I knew him better than anyone else had. Perhaps our work together had only made small indentations in his character, but I had the strong feeling that any further working through was beyond our ability, despite having met analytically for quite a few years. I don't regard this as analytic failure so much as pointing to the real limitations and our need to acknowledge and accept those limitations of our work with certain character organizations (Cooper, 2016).

Discussion

Some patients live their lives without subjective involvement. They are animated and appear to interact with others, but are neither simply alive nor dead in the terms analysts often speak of. These individuals have been described in the literature in multiple ways, but within the clinical situation, all have in common the feeling of a non-human existence. While they share features of both narcissistic and schizoid characters, it is meaningful that they do not fit neatly into either of these categories and have consequently been described as 'as-if', 'normopathic' and 'normotic' terms that reflect their *seeming* to be a person.

If one accepts the existence of a death instinct then the familiar trope of the alive analyst helping to bring the dead patient to life becomes problematic. For if there is a death instinct, then it exists for the analyst as it does for the patient.

What I have tried to illustrate here is that it may be valuable for the analyst to have contact with the forms of affect and mentation that mark experiences of deadness, to move in and out and between those spaces analytically, so as to speak with the patient from a place that recognizes a common longing, the nostalgia that Baudrillard (2000) spoke to. In order to speak with patients from these states, the analyst may first have to struggle with and confront a variety of frightening feelings, including envy of the patient's non-human existence.

Viewing the topic of psychic life and death in dichotomous terms may lead analysts to overlook their own attraction to states of mind that seem to promise a release from the human condition. From my perspective, the analyst is not simply engaged in bringing the patient to life so much as attempting to reestablish the dialectic relationship between life and death instincts within the patient.

Notes

1 Of course, it is not the brain so much as the mind that I am referring to, but for the purpose of making this comparison, I am taking some license. The attack is on the analyst's mind and may be likened to what Freud (1905) and later Klein (1933) regarded as the cannibalistic quality of infantile life.
2 While I write that the patient's self had been annihilated by this force, I do not mean that it had completely vanished. In line with what I am suggesting regarding a living deadness, I would say enough libido existed to animate his deadness, but not enough to constitute subjective aliveness. In other words, he experienced libido in the service of the death instinct, rather than the dialectical interpenetration of these forces.

References

Abel-Hirsch, N. (2010). 'The Life Instinct.' *International Journal of Psychoanalysis*, 91(5): 1055–1071.
Baudrillard, J. (2000). 'The Final Solution: Cloning Beyond the Human and Inhuman.' In: *The Vital Illusion*. New York: Columbia University Press Books, pp. 1–30.
Bion, W.R. (1959). 'Attacks on Linking.' *International Journal of Psycho-Analysis*, 40: 308–315.
Bion, W.R. (1970). *Attention and Interpretation*. London: Tavistock Publications.
Bollas, C. (1987). *The Shadow of the Object*. London: Free Association Press.
Bromberg, P.M. (2011). *The Shadow of the Tsunami and the Growth of the Relational Mind*. New York: Routledge.
Chalmers, D. (1996). *The Conscious Mind: In Search of a Fundamental Theory*. New York and Oxford: Oxford University Press.
Cooper, S.H. (2016). *The Analyst's Experience of the Depressive Position: The Melancholic Errand of Psychoanalysis*. New York: Routledge.
Deutsch, H. (1942). 'Some Forms of Emotional Disturbance and Their Relationship to Schizophrenia.' *Psychoanalytic Quarterly*, 11: 301–321.
Freud, S. (1905). 'Three Essays on Sexuality.' *S.E.*, Vol. 7, London: Hogarth Press, pp. 130–243.
Freud, S. (1920). 'Beyond the Pleasure Principle.' *S.E.*, Vol. 18, London: Hogarth Press, pp. 3–64.

Freud, S. (1923). 'The Ego and the Id.' *S.E.*, Vol. 19, London: Hogarth Press, pp. 1–66.
Freud, S. (1924). 'The Economic Problem of Masochism.' *S.E.*, Vol. 19, London: Hogarth Press, pp. 155–170.
Freud, S. (1930). 'Civilization and Its Discontents.' *S.E.*, Vol. 21, London: Hogarth Press, pp. 59–145.
Freud, S. (1937). 'Analysis Terminable and Interminable.' *S.E.*, Vol. 23, London: Hogarth Press, pp. 209–253.
Green, A. (1999). 'The Intuition of the Negative in *Playing and Reality*.' In: G. Kohon (Ed.) *The Dead Mother: The Work of Andre Green*, New York: Routledge, pp. 205–221.
Greenberg, J.R. & Mitchell, S.A. (1983). *Object Relations in Psychoanalytic Theory*. Cambridge, MA: Harvard University Press.
Haraway, D. (1990). *Simians, Cyborgs, Women: The Reinvention of Nature*. New York: Routledge.
Kernberg, O. (2009). 'The Concept of the Death Drive: A Clinical Perspective.' *International Journal of Psychoanalysis*, 90: 1009–1023.
Klein, M. (1933). 'The Early Development of Conscience in the Child.' In: Roger Money-Kyrle (Ed.) *Love, Guilt and Reparation and Other Works*. London: Vintage, 1998.
Kohon, G. (1999). *No Lost Certainties to Be Recovered*. London: Karnac Books.
Laplanche, J. & Pontalis, J.B. (1967). *The Language of Psychoanalysis*. Donald Nicholson-Smith (Trans.). London: Hogarth Press, 1973.
McDougall, J. (1978). *Plea for a Measure of Abnormality*. London: Free Association Books, 1990.
McDougall, J. (1982). *Theatres of the Mind: Illusion and Truth on the Psychoanalytic Stage*. London: Free Association Books, 1986.
Ogden, T.H. (1980). 'On the Nature of Schizophrenic Conflict.' *International Journal of Psycho-Analysis*, 61: 513–533.
Ogden, T.H. (1982). 'Treatment of the Schizophrenic State of Non-Experience.' In: L.B. Boyer & P.L. Giovaccini (Eds.) *Technical Factors in the Treatment of the Severely Disturbed Patient*. New York: Jason Aronson, pp. 217–260.
Ogden, T.H. (1989). *The Primitive Edge of Experience*. Northvale, NJ: Jason Aronson.
Ogden, T.H. (1994). *Subjects of Analysis*. Northvale, NJ: Jason Aronson.
Ogden, T.H. (1997). 'Analyzing Forms of Aliveness and Deadness.' In: T.H. Ogden (Ed.) *Reverie and Interpretation: Sensing Something Human*. Northvale, NJ: Jason Aronson, pp. 23–63.
Searles, H. (1960). *The Non-Human Environment in Normal Development and in Schizophrenia*. New York: International Universities Press.
Segal, H. (1997). 'On the Clinical Usefulness of the Concept of the Death Instinct.' In: John Steiner (Ed.) *Psychoanalysis, Literature and War*. New York: Routledge, pp. 17–26.
Shoshani, M. (2009). *Dare to Be Human*. New York: Routledge.
Symington, N. (1983). 'The Analyst's Act of Freedom as Agent of Therapeutic Change.' *International Review of Psycho-Analysis*, 10: 283–291.
Winnicott, D.W. (1965a). 'Ego Distortion in Terms of True and False Self.' In: D.W. Winnicott (Ed.) *Maturational Processes and the Facilitating Environment*. Madison, CT: International Universities Press, pp. 140–152.
Winnicott, D.W. (1965b). 'The Theory of Infant-Parent Relationship.' In: D.W. Winnicott (Ed.) *Maturational Processes and the Facilitating Environment*. Madison, CT: International Universities Press, pp. 17–55.

Chapter 4

Symbiont life

Donald arrived at my office for a series of consultations. He was a successful Wall Street lawyer, some 10 or 12 years younger than me, and made a good initial impression in appearing casually amiable. He'd been happily married to a woman called Claire for several years, but now things had changed. He reported that he felt downright miserable. Over the course of our consultation meetings, I learned that despite Claire's remarkable success in her professional field, and her achievements which placed her in a rarified group, Donald yearned to leave the marriage in order to find another partner, someone who he thought was more appropriate for him; someone, he said, who would be the 'right choice'. Given his own professional achievements, I found this a curious complaint. Furthermore, Donald and Claire travelled together, entertained, had a wide-ranging group of friends and had raised two children. I felt I was missing something, that something wasn't quite right. It was partly this feeling that led me to suggest that he consider entering an analysis.

I learned over the next several months that Donald had been quite taken with Claire during their courtship, but that his attraction had turned to a feeling of disgust. Since having children, Claire had gained weight. This was not uncommon, but seemed so unattractive to Donald that he despised being with her. He felt enormous pressure to get out of the marriage as soon as possible, even if it meant losing the house and his assets. Had he brought up his dissatisfaction with Claire, I wondered? No, he imagined this would only anger her and result in her not taking him seriously. How much weight did he estimate Claire had gained since having children? At least 7–10 lbs, he said. This completely changed how he thought of her. He felt he couldn't hold her in the esteem he previously had. Her legs and arms were thicker, and he found her back fat repellent. The only solution, he thought, was to leave her and find an athletic woman with large breasts who would be physically attractive to him. This was the sort of woman he had always imagined being with, the sort of woman he felt he deserved.

I wondered with Donald if there was something else pushing him out of the marriage and asked him to consider the emotional toll of his actions on himself and his family before acting precipitously. Donald was not able to consider that his dissatisfaction had anything to do with himself and his own wishes, fantasies or frustrations. And he denied that his feelings had anything to do with Claire becoming a mother or had any connection to memories of his own mother and her body. He saw no benefit in speaking about the past and rarely would reference his childhood experiences or his family – they were not the issue after all; it was his marriage that had brought him to see me, and it was Claire he had been having such a difficult time with. He insisted that there was nothing but Claire's appearance that felt intolerable to him. Yes, he had dreaded spending time with her alone or in public and was no longer interested in what she had to say, but this was solely the result of his feelings regarding her appearance. Undeterred by any nostalgia he had for their life lived together, or any present sense of connection to Claire, their relationship or family, Donald went about serving her with divorce papers, moved out of their home and into an apartment, with what I considered alarming alacrity, but which for him brought near immediate relief.

Donald's stunning lack of self-reflectiveness and shallow concern for others as whole objects concerned me. As this drama unfolded, I experienced a series of further unsettling incidents. I must stress that these experiences did not all happen at the same time, but seemed to have a cumulative effect. When I would go to the patient waiting area, sometimes Donald would not be there. Instead, I would find him in my other colleague's empty offices looking around at the objects on their desks, or out of the window at the view. He seemed to think nothing of walking into someone else's office, even though the door was partially closed. At other times, when I went to collect him, I'd find him with his head in the suite's refrigerator, looking over the contents, sometimes helping himself to juice or water. Not infrequently when I was still with the patient before his hour, I would hear Donald enter the suite, slam the front door, loudly swing open the door to the restroom, and yank up the toilet seat so loudly I heard 'crack' from inside my office. This behaviour continued once he'd entered my consulting room. Donald would turn off lights he preferred not be on without asking my permission. It also became a matter of habit for him to completely empty his pockets before laying on the couch, spilling coins, his phone, slips of paper and anything else he had onto the table before settling in to discuss issues at work or in his dating life. He wasn't interested in thinking through the problems he brought into treatment. Rather, he wanted me to tell him what to do. He was very concerned that he make 'the right decision' and quite anxious about making 'the wrong decision'. He wanted surety, and he thought I had it. It was simple. I should just tell him whether to continue dating a particular woman, or whether to switch firms in order to make more money or how he should respond to his parents when they liked, or failed to like, something on his social media accounts. I was to tell him what 'the right decision' was, and he would do that.

He seemed not to register that his behaviours were aggressive and transgressed boundaries. Indeed, his manner became overly cordial and familiar in a way that paralleled his physical actions. Over time, Donald began to refer to us as 'friends' and then to me as his 'buddy'. He determined on his own that I lived in Brooklyn and what neighbourhood I lived in. Knowing several restaurants in that area, he began asking if I went to particular spots. Maybe he'd see me there, he said. Donald also began commenting on the way I was dressed: 'Nice shirt, I like that shirt buddy; are you going to take me shopping with you?' 'Hey, buddy, when are we going clothes shopping together?' Such questions became frequent refrains at the beginning of our sessions, and after attempting to explore the patient's fantasy of us going clothes shopping together to little benefit, I remained quiet when he asked. The questions took on something of a feeling of a ritual that Donald would perform at the beginning of his sessions.

Countertransferentially, the effect on me was insidious. I felt guilty not answering his constant questions about us shopping together or being able to productively explore them in order to determine their underlying meaning or intended effect. While I didn't name it, I felt assaulted by his relation to the physical objects in the suite: the front door, the toilet, the lights he would turn on or off or the surfaces he would occupy. As a result, I could not find a space for reverie in the sessions, or access the dreamlike associative process that connected me with my own inner life. I often feel welcoming when my patients enter my consulting room but Donald's entry provoked anxiety. Indeed, it felt that this was only the conscious portion of my reaction to my patient, but that his effect on me was even more far reaching, as I noticed one night while out with my wife for dinner that I was anxiously looking around the restaurant, dreading that I might see Donald there or, perhaps more precisely, that he might see me there.

Winnicott's (1947) paper on hate in the countertransference was helpful to me, as I read about how the analyst working with such patients 'must be prepared to bear strain without expecting the patient to know anything about what he is doing, perhaps over a long period of time'. Winnicott said that in order to do this, the analyst needs to be aware of his own fear and hatred for his patient, but this didn't feel like a problem for me. Yet as helpful as this consultation felt, Winnicott wrote something else that felt even more specific to my experience, that

> acknowledgement cannot be expected because at the primitive root of the patient that is being looked for there is no capacity for identification with the analyst, and certainly the patient cannot see that the analyst's hate is often engendered by the very things the patient does in his crude way of loving.

Most certainly, Donald couldn't understand his engendering my own hate through what Winnicott perfectly called a 'crude way of loving'. It made sense to me that Donald had engendered an experience of hate within me and that this was an experience that in some way he needed (me to feel).

It was Winnicott's statement that patients such as this had 'no capacity for identification with the analyst' that caught my attention and felt relevant. Normally, I understand my work to be guided by my own unconscious, in what Diamond (2011) has called the analyst's 'analytic mind use'. By this he means his recognition and utilization of his mental activities, including the unconscious, somatized and less-self-reflectively accessible derivatives, which form symbolizing and representational interpretations, create containment and allow the analyst to clarify, reflect on, elaborate and validate comments. The use the analyst makes of his mind, often operating outside of the patient or the analyst's conscious awareness, allows the patient to unconsciously *use* the analyst's mental activities. Diamond (2011) writes, 'When the patient unconsciously experiences and identifies with the analyst's inner psychic work geared towards more deeply understanding the patient, something rather mysterious happens, resulting in the patient' learning a new way to relate to his/her own mind' (p. 209). But Donald didn't seem to be identifying with the ways in which I used, or attempted to use, these capacities when I was with him. As Winnicott suggested, he didn't seem capable of that.

Spezzano (2007) has similarly suggested that patients need to find a home in the analyst's mind, by which he means that the patient needs to experience the analyst's mind as a place in which the patient exists as an internal object. Much like Diamond, Spezzano understood therapeutic action to result from the patient's unconscious identification not only with the analyst's interpreting function but also his ability or capacity to think. He writes, 'This identification emerges out of the patient's sense of the analyst's mind as a place where the patient and the analyst are related in a way that includes the analyst's thinking with agency and freedom about the patient'. As a regular part of analytic treatment, symbiont relations are common, as exemplified by Spezzano's discussion of two patients who found a home in his mind. In reading his description of these patients existing as internal objects in his mind, one has the feeling that Spezzano welcomed them there, as any analyst might welcome deep engagement with their analysand. Thus at a conscious level, there is a position of openness the analyst adopts, one that allows for the positive growth of the patient through allowing themselves to be affected by the patient and make the patient and her objects a part of the analyst's own inner life. These are the more benign forms of symbiont living that we regularly encounter in a treatment relationship. The unconscious relation with the analyst may assume a similar benign form (as, for instance, is described in Chapter 2 wherein the analyst dreams aspects of the patient's inner world that are inaccessible to them) or may take on a more malignant character. To continue to use Spezzano's metaphor, if the analyst offers a home for the mind, then I felt that Donald had broken into my home and that if he took up residence there it was a home invasion (Director, 2014) which deprived me of agency and freedom of thought.

Donald existed in a state prior to his being able to form identifications, a state similar to that described by Meltzer (1975) as one of adhesive identification, where the individual mimics rather than takes in the qualities of the other. Additionally, my own adoption of the analytic stance had opened me to taking in portions of my patient I found difficult to metabolize and return. Fliess (1942) wrote of the analyst's introjecting his patient transiently, taking in portions of his patient's experience as the analyst's own. He described 'step[ping] into his [the patient's] shoes and obtain[ing] in this way an inside knowledge that is almost first hand' (p. 212). The use of what Fliess regarded as a transient experience of empathy was to help the analyst to better understand his patient. But, as both Brown (2011) and de M'Uzan (1989) have observed, Fliess also cautioned that this process may become a situation of danger.[1] Within the regressed state of the transference-countertransference, the analyst 'becomes the subject himself' (p. 215) as the patient's instinctual tendencies having been introjected by the analyst, become his own narcissistic tendencies. De M'Uzan (1989, p. 84) writes,

> By withdrawing the most individual aspects of his own personality, the analyst allows his analysand to invade him. He thereby creates the conditions in which the patient's representation, which is now acquiring considerable power, can occupy him and, at the same time, become the object of a narcissistic cathexis. The menace hanging over the stability of the psychoanalyst's sense of identity now becomes clearer. The boundaries between outside and inside tend to disappear. One could almost say that we are in fact faced with no longer knowing quite who is who.

I began to have the conviction, in the form of a terrorizing fantasy, that his invasion of my space, the space of my office suite and the space of my mind, was his primitive attempt, through mimesis, *to become me*. Reminiscent of the film *Freaky Friday* (2003), Donald would be me, and I would be him. I would be filled with feelings of anxiety and hatred, and my self-experience (i.e. my thinking and reflections) would be emptied out, while he would make himself at home in my office, throwing down the contents of his pockets as he would the split-off contents of his mind for me to keep, hold, treat as my own. Looking back on the experience I can see I was in the grip of an unconscious enactment. However, I was unable to use this fantasy therapeutically, as its powerful effect was to hijack me, my sense of identity and my capacities as an analyst.

By creating in me experiences of guilt, confusion, shame, assault, invasion and paranoia he had shown me what he was unable to say about the conditions of his internal world – or to put it another way – what it was like to be him amongst his internal objects. I was made to experience assaults on objects I valued and thought of as my own – my room, clothes and possessions, just as Donald had experienced changes in his wife, Claire, as assaults on something which he thought he owned. In introducing the term projective identification Melanie Klein (1946) described the projection of 'bad parts of the self [. . .] meant not only to injure but also to control and to take possession of the object' (p. 102). She considered this sort of relation a precursor of an aggressive object relation. Describing projective identification some years later, Thomas Ogden writes of the analyst unconsciously 'enter[ing] into a form of negation of himself as a separate I' and that 'the recipient of the projective identification becomes a participant in the negation of himself as a separate subject, thus making 'psychological room' in himself to be (in unconscious fantasy) occupied (taken over) by the projector' (p. 100). That Ogden (1994) and de M'Uzan (1989) use similar words to describe the potential danger associated with this terrifying process, attests to its power and to the analyst's vulnerability to 'being swept along by the irresistible frightening lure of an unfolding

52 Symbiont life

horror story' (Ogden, 1994, p. 105). Thus it would appear both de M'Uzan and Ogden regard this process as a vehicle by which the analyst allows an unconscious occupation of himself by the other so that he can think about something the patient cannot.

The process was also described as one of 'therapeutic symbiosis' by Harold Searles (1979) who wrote,

> For the deepest levels of therapeutic interaction to be reached, both patient and therapist must experience a temporary breaching of the ego boundaries which demarcate each participant from the other. In this state there occurs ... a temporary introjection, by the therapist, of the patient's pathogenic conflicts; the therapist thus deals with these at an intrapsychic, unconscious as well as conscious level, bringing to bear upon them the capacities of his own relatively strong ego. Then, similarly by introjection, the patient benefits from this intrapsychic therapeutic work which has been accomplished in the therapist.
>
> (p. 520)

Both Rosenfeld (2005) and Bion (1965) wrote of parasitic object relating, differentiating it from projective identification in both intensity and duration. It felt quite right to me to describe this relation as one of symbiosis, which essentially means 'living together'. Donald's relation with me seemed to be similar to one of endosymbiosis, whereby the endosymbiont lacks a nutrient the host can provide and its contact with the host leads to the stimulation of specialized cells (what in psychoanalysis we might call the capacity to think), which can then be reabsorbed. While this relation is one biologist would call 'facultative' or optional, as neither party's survival depended upon the coupling, I would argue that as far as Donald's nascent psychic life was concerned the symbiosis was 'obligate' and depended upon a type of parasitic connection to me. Donald's breaking in, in other words, was the only way he could communicate. And his assumption of my identity was an early attempt at relating in the absence of the ability to identify.

Approximately 18 months into the treatment, Donald was talking about a woman he'd been dating. She was a fashion model and considerably younger than himself. He described how she had a different kind of body than the type he normally lusted after. She was lithe but small breasted, Donald continued, whereas he had been fantasizing about a thin woman with large breasts. He said this was 'perfect ... a perfect body'. As he was speaking, I had the first reverie-like experience I can recall with him. I started thinking about nudes painted by the sixteenth-century artist, Peter Paul Rubens, the contours of their bodies and the colours. Eventually, my thoughts went to Plato and his notion that there existed ideal forms. This led to thoughts about how my patient Donald also had the notion that there was an ideal body type and that this was not simply a preference. I could feel within myself the concrete aspects of his thinking, the limits of imagining that had been such a familiar part of my work with him when, in an unbidden flash, I heard Grace Jones singing a song from the 1980s. I did not think about this song or the singer, but I heard her deep and powerful voice declaring, 'I'm not perfect, but I'm perfect for you'. This chorus (which is the title of the song) repeated several times. I thought it was curious that I could not recall any other lyrics. I was startled by this experience as I had not yet been able to access my usual flow of associations, at least not in a way that felt comfortably my own. I would contrast this with my previous experience in the restaurant with my wife, where the association was more nightmarish. But what I felt sitting together with my patient, hearing Grace Jones, did not feel like an assault or an invasion or as if its purpose was to create anxiety.

I had previously felt that Donald was not able to receive verbal communications from me, that communication could only flow in one direction, from the patient to the analyst, and therefore my psychic orientation had to allow this to occur until he became receptive (Joseph, 1989; Di Ceglie, 2013). I took my internal experience as a sign that it may now be possible and asked Donald whether he had ever heard of Grace Jones.

He sat bolt upright on the couch, turned around and looked at me strangely. He asked why I was asking him that. I told him the title of the song in my mind and that it was popular in the 1980s. He'd never heard of the song and didn't take up the meaning of the title. But he said he was looking at pictures of her on the Internet the night before our session. He laid back down and told me he was trying to get a sense of what was attractive about a model's body, why other people would find that kind of body attractive, so he was googling pictures of models and came across photos of Grace Jones. He described how he was arrested by her look. He had been too young to know who she was but when he saw her on the computer he was captivated.

'She had a very aggressive thing going on', I said.

'Yes! That was it *exactly*. I love that', he exclaimed.

I immediately thought of Donald asking me whether his decisions were right or wrong. What I felt for the first time was the enormity of the helplessness underlying his confusion. Rather than feel helpless myself, in the countertransference, I understood Donald's underlying helplessness, which led to his attempts to control his objects in the only ways he could imagine.

What Winnicott (1950–5) would call the patient's primitive love impulse was evident now in speech:

> Yet still exist[ed] in a realm when ego growth is only starting, when integration . . . is not an established fact . . . when there is not yet a capacity for taking responsibility . . . [when] there is not even ruthlessness; it is a pre-ruth era, and if destruction could be part of the aim in the id impulse, then destruction is only incidental to id satisfaction.
>
> (p. 210)

The significance of my own reverie-like experience indicated something he had not been able to think about but which could now be thought of as an experience of the individual.

It seems to me that especially with patients like Donald, there is a necessity for an initial period in the treatment when the analyst will feel invaded, taken over, kidnapped or negated before he is able to apply the use of his own mind to the patient's primitive projected psychic contents. Michael Parsons (2014) recently wrote of the

> need for an analyst to let the internal world of a patient impinge on the analyst's internal world. This is not just so that the analyst's countertransference can be observed safely and instructively. The analyst has to allow it to happen in a way that does *not* feel safe. Patients are helped to change by knowing, consciously or unconsciously, that they are with someone who is open unconditionally to whatever impact the patient may have on them.
>
> (p. 221)

During the period of therapeutic symbiosis, when I had introjected the patient's conflicts and was unconsciously working on them, I could not dream (in Bion's sense of the term). The resolution of this intrapsychic work, resulting in an experience of 'figurability' (Botellas, 2005), arising from the intersubjective interplay of two unconscious processes, allowed me to use my mind associatively, alongside the patient's, rather than feel invaded or controlled. The reverie I experienced while sitting with the patient was evidence that Donald's unprocessed emotional experience was transformed through a symbiotic process into a thought.

Bion (1970) referred to this experience as 'being-at-one with the psychic reality of the patient'. Indeed, it is an intimacy that is itself transformative, even prior to the delivery of observation or interpretation. Bion (1967) wrote,

> I think that what the patient is saying and what the interpretation is (which you give), is in a sense relatively unimportant. Because by the time you are able to give a patient an interpretation which the patient understands, all the work has been done.

For Ogden (2015), this means that

> the analyst and the patient have already been changed by the experience of jointly intuiting the unsettling psychic reality with which they have been at one. The experience of coming to terms with, being at one with, a formerly unthinkable psychic reality changes both patient and analyst.

For Ogden, as for Bion, the interpretation is, therefore, 'superfluous'.

Note

1 It is striking to note the widespread caution that accompanies this necessary but potentially dangerous aspect of the treatment. Baranger and Baranger (2008, p. 809) from the River Plate tradition also note the analyst's introjection of the patient's objects and qualities of the patient's self-experience, but they seem less open to tolerating these than some other authors, noting, 'this introjective aspect has to be limited and controlled to avoid feelings in the analyst of being inundated by the situation (as sometimes happens, especially with psychotic patients who try to inject their madness into the analyst)'.

References

Baranger, M. & Baranger, W. (2008). 'The Analytic Situation as a Dynamic Field.' *International Journal of Psychoanalysis*, 89: 795–826.
Bion, W. (1965). *Transformations*. London: Heinemann.
Bion, W. (1967). 'First Seminar – 12 April 1967.' In: J. Aguayo & B. Malin (Eds.) *Wilfred Bion: Los Angeles Seminars and Supervision*. London: Karnac Books, 2013, pp. 1–31.
Bion, W. (1970). *Attention and Interpretation*. London: Maresfield.
Botella, S. & Botella, C. (2005). *The Work of Psychic Figurability: Mental States Without Representation*. New York: Routledge.
Brown, L.J. (2011). *Intersubjective Processes and the Unconscious*. New York: Routledge.
De M'Uzan, M. (1989). 'During the Session: Considerations on the Analyst's Mental Functioning.' In: *Death and Identity: Being and the Psycho-Sexual Drama*. London: Karnac Books, 2013, pp. 79–97.
Diamond, M. (2011). 'The Impact of the Mind of the Analyst: From Unconscious Process to Intrapsychic Change.' In: M. Diamond & C. Christian (Eds.) *The Second Century of Psychoanalysis: Evolving Perspectives on Therapeutic Action*. London: Karnac Books, pp. 205–235.
Di Ceglie, G.R. (2013). 'Orientation, Containment and the Emergence of Symbolic Thinking.' *International Journal of Psychoanalysis*, 94: 1077–1091.
Director, L. (2014). 'The Object Invades: Illustration and Implications.' *Contemporary Psychoanalysis*, 50(3), 437–458.
Fliess, W. (1942). 'The Metapsychology of the Analyst.' *Psychoanalytic Quarterly*, 11: 211–227.
Joseph, B. (1975). 'The Patient Who Is Difficult to Reach.' In: M. Feldman & E.G. Spillius (Eds.) *Psychic Equilibrium and Psychic Change: Selected Papers of Betty Joseph*. London: Routledge, 1989, pp. 75–87.
Klein, M. (1946). 'Notes on Some Schizoid Mechanisms.' *International Journal of Psychoanalysis*, 27: 99–110.
Meltzer, D. (1975). 'Adhesive Identification.' *Contemporary Psycho-Analysis*, 11: 289–310.
Ogden, T.H. (1994). *Subjects of Analysis*. New York: Jason Aronson.
Ogden, T.H. (2015). 'Intuiting the Truth of What's Happening: On Bion's "Notes on Memory and Desire".' *Psychoanalytic Quarterly*, 84(2): 285–306.
Parsons, M. (2014). *Living Psychoanalysis*. New York: Routledge.
Rosenfeld, H. (2005). *Impasse and Interpretation*. New York: Routledge.

Searles, H.F. (1979). 'Transitional Phenomena and Therapeutic Symbiosis.' In: *Countertransference and Related Subjects*. New York: International Universities Press, 1999, pp. 503–576.

Spezzano, C. (2007). 'A Home for the Mind.' *Psychoanalytic Quarterly*, 76S: 1563–1583.

Winnicott, D.W. (1947). 'Hate in the Countertransference.' In: *Through Paediatrics to Psycho-Analysis*. New York: Brunner Mazel, 1992, pp. 194–203.

Winnicott, D.W. (1950–5). 'Aggression in Relation to Emotional Development.' In: *Through Paediatrics to Psycho-Analysis*. New York: Brunner Mazel, 1992, pp. 204–218.

Chapter 5

Performative and enactive features of psychoanalytic witnessing
The transference as the scene of address

From its inception, psychoanalysis has made central the study of memory and repetition. Freud's (1895b) early investigations with Breuer in *Studies on Hysteria* concerned themes of remembering and repeating which, despite subsequent development and increasing complexity in psychoanalytic theory, remain at the centre of analytic clinical enterprise. While remembering has often been posed in opposition to repeating, and favoured over it, following Loewald (1965), I will argue that the relationship between the two is more complex, particularly in work with traumatized patients.

This chapter will attempt to broaden the concept of 'witnessing' to incorporate the traumatized patient developing a capacity for witnessing, as well as a witnessing that occurs within the analytic relationship itself. Following classical texts that refused to separate repeating from remembering, I will argue that the patient's trauma resides in the transference-countertransference matrix through various forms of action performed and enacted in the dyad. These actions create a scene of traumatic (re)occurrence, which is intended to communicate experience to an *other*. The unique context of the psychoanalytic encounter is what allows traumatic repetition to take on the quality of an address rather than remain meaningless reproduction.

To begin, I would like to briefly differentiate the conception of enactive witnessing from the subject of enactment, which has become a mainstay of contemporary discussions concerning therapeutic action. I conceive of psychoanalytic witnessing as a living-out of traumatic experience in the consulting room and not as the expression of warded-off dissociated self-states. My use of the term 'enactive' (Reis, 2009a, 2009 b, 2010; BCPSG, 2013) differs from the conception of enactment that has been favoured and made a cornerstone of relational approaches to the treatment of traumatized individuals. The former is a procedural, embodied representation outside of words and not captured in images, aligned with conceptions of implicit relational knowing (Stern et al., 1998; Lyons-Ruth, 1998). As such, it is present in the treatment of traumatized individuals but not restricted to trauma, and it is not conceived of as being dissociatively based (Nahum, 2017). Grossmark (2018), who has utilized the enactive conception in his idea of enactive co-narration, has also differentiated this idea from relational enactment as described by Stern (2010). Citing Stern, Grossmark (2018, p. 129) wrote, '[He] describes the "narrative freedom" that emerges in a "continuous productive unfolding"' (pp. 116–118) as the treatment progresses. From Stern's perspective, this productive process is interrupted by enactment. Enactment occurs when a dissociated state in the patient 'calls out a dissociated or not-me state in the analyst' (p. 121). This is a mutual enactment that rigidifies clinical relatedness and 'interrupts each person's capacity to serve as witness for the other'; 'events remain coded in procedural terms, in action' (p. 123). From my own perspective of enactive witnessing, as well as Grossmark's (p. 121) perspective of enactive co-narration,

> these enactments are not seen as interruptions in the unfolding narrative but are the emergence of narrative in the register of non-representation. In other words, what is being represented is the failure of representation itself along with the content of that failed representation. The narrative does continue to emerge but in the register of action – eloquent or otherwise – in the procedural and somatic.
>
> (Grossmark, 2018, p. 129)

My approach shares much with Bromberg's (2011a), who emphasizes the role of unconscious communication in his conception of enactment. Like Bromberg, I see this communication occurring via subsymbolic channels occurring in a transference-countertransference field, and like Bromberg, I place primary emphasis on the internal experiences of the analyst in this communicative process. By leaving rational thought behind and making the 'material' of the session the phenomenological experiences of the analyst from moment to moment, we both believe the analyst gains access to an aspect of the patient's experience that has not found meaningful expression. However, my approach also differs from Bromberg's in a number of important ways. Bromberg relies on a dissociative model of the mind to ground his understanding of these phenomena, and I do not. As mentioned earlier, enactive representation is not conceptualized as occurring within dissociative self-states and is not experienced by the individual as a 'not-me' experience. Whereas dissociative self-states already exist as psychic experience, enactive experience is rooted in the body, and as Freud (1917, p. 258) noted, would need to make a 'puzzling leap' in order to be transformed into psychic experience (though as I will made clear I do not believe the goal of working with such bodily experience necessarily involves making that leap). To this point, I see the ultimate aims of my analytic approach to be different from those Bromberg envisions. For instance, Bromberg (Chefetz & Bromberg, 2004, pp. 412–413) writes, 'The goal is dyadic, here-and-now reconstruction of this activity in such subjective detail that the patient's dissociated self-states, being affectively enacted as "not me" elements in their relationship, become symbolically processed as part of "me"'. My aim throughout this volume is to illustrate that people improve in psychoanalysis not due to the symbolization of defensively warded-off experience that can now be felt as part of oneself, but rather from having an experience of being with an *other* that very often cannot be adequately captured or narrated by way of the symbolic and does not have to do with expanding the ego's claim over experience. Because my views differ from Bromberg's in these regards, I do not discard psychoanalytic conceptions of unconscious phantasy as Bromberg (2011a) does, nor do I agree with his position (Bromberg, 2011b) that disclosure by the analyst of his countertransference thoughts and feelings is not simply permissible but necessary.

Enactive witnessing involves memory in what Loewald (1976) termed its enactive rather than representational form. The goal of psychoanalytic witnessing is to allow and witness memory in its varied forms, without attempting to symbolize or make personally understandable the experience – to accept the experience of the trauma without therapeutic ambition. The analyst occupying the position of witness understands that performative and enactive features of traumatic experience are not to be simply translated or transduced into symbolic form. Part of the integrity of the experience of trauma is itself a wordless registration. I do not wish to imply by this statement that the analyst is unable to engage with the experience of the patient's trauma; in fact, I will argue quite the opposite.

The centrality of action in memory phenomena

It is the unintegrative quality of traumatic memory that marks traumatic experience. Laub (1992a) has suggested that massive trauma precludes its own registration. While it has become commonplace to note that traumatic memory resists symbolization and presents as fragmented, iconic and sensorial phenomena, psychoanalytic investigation of its enactive qualities has received considerably less attention. However, Freud (1895b) understood this crucial aspect of traumatic memory and focused attention on its non-conscious form as well as its quality as an *action*. For Freud, memory in hysterical neurosis was linked to motor reaction: 'An uninterrupted series, extending from the unmodified mnemonic residues of affective experiences and acts of thought to the hysterical symptoms, which are the mnemonic symbols of those experiences and thoughts' (p. 295). When he and Breuer addressed the motor phenomena of hysterical attacks, they wrote that these 'can be interpreted partly as universal forms of reaction appropriate to the affect accompanying the memory . . . partly as a *direct expression of these memories*' (Breuer & Freud, 1893, p. 15, my italics).

Later, the notion of the mnemonic trace, which Freud hypothesized as the registration of a perception in non-conscious memory, extended past the description of hysterical pathology to describe the normal function of non-traumatic memory. Over the course of his writing, Freud (1895a, 1900, 1925) would rely on the notion of the mnemonic trace, attempting in the *Project for a Scientific Psychology* (1895a) to describe the neuronal inscriptions of affective experiences which remain out of conscious awareness (i.e. unconscious memories). These inscriptions were described not as residing in any one neuron, but as distributed in the relationships between neurons, in what today would be called neural networks. Thus memory as conceived in the *Project* was not a cognitive function performed by a conscious subject, but a presubjective physiological change experienced outside of the awareness of the conscious subject.

Freud's approach to viewing motor response as a form of memory finds validation in contemporary cognitive science. The distributed mnemonic traces he described are more recently described as 'enactive' (Bruner et al., 1966), 'subsymbolic' (Bucci, 1997), 'procedural' (Clyman, 1991) and 'implicit' (Lyons-Ruth, 1998) encoding of information. Within contemporary psychoanalysis, this presymbolic, sensory mode of experiencing has led to concepts of self-experiencing which emphasize rhythm and contiguity at the level of sensory impression (Ogden, 1989). These experiences are memory without form, which, just as they inform, fall back into indeterminacy (Clough, 2007).

Freud (1914) also described the enactive qualities of patients reliving trauma in the clinical setting: 'He reproduces it not as a memory, but as an action; he *repeats* it, without, of course, knowing that he is repeating it' (p. 150, original italics). Freud demonstrated that the patient was not repeating a dissociated or repressed memory but rather that the *action* of repetition itself was a phenomenon of memory: 'As long as the patient is in the treatment he cannot escape from this compulsion to repeat; and in the end we understand that this is his way of remembering' (1914, p. 150). This insight never left Freud's work, as illustrated by the fact that, when later describing what I have termed the enactive quality of memory, he observed that the patient will repeat his 'modes of reaction . . . right before our eyes' (1937, p. 341) – a fact which he attributed prime importance to as constituting 'half our analytic task'. Loewald (1965) noted that Freud considered repetitive actions a form of memory, as described earlier and that additionally remembering was seen as an act of repeating, as a 'reproduction in the psychical field' (Freud, 1914, p. 153).

Analytic witnessing

The witnessing function of the analyst has been explored by several writers. Orange (1995) considers it one of the self-object functions, that the witnessing presence of the analyst as 'a responsive person' makes recognition and affective experiencing of past traumas possible for patients who may never have experienced the meaning and articulation of their traumatic histories. According to Orange, witnessing facilitates both the experiencing and remembering of trauma:

> [It] undoes shame and restores the positive valuation of the self. It establishes and maintains self-experience, and it clearly deserves designation as a 'self-object' function. In cases of post-traumatic stress, witnessing is one form the emotional availability of the analyst must take.
>
> (1995, p. 140)

Poland (2000) describes emotional immediacy on the part of the analyst, which is at once silent but active, engaged rather than abstinent. For Poland, a partial detachment on the part of the analyst exists side by side with his deep caring, and his observations as a separate other exist alongside his participatory interaction in a painful experience. Poland differentiates the witnessing presence of the analyst from therapeutic attempts to interpret, or to provide comfort or the alleviation of suffering. 'Recognition, not exoneration', he writes, 'is what is called for' (p. 20). While the position of clinical witnessing described by Poland is meant to apply to all analyses, Grand (2000) adopts a very similar clinical position in her treatment of the severely traumatized, noting the intimate separation between analyst and patient:

> The trauma survivor remains solitary in the moment of her own extinction. No one knew her in the moment when she died without dying; no one knows her now, in her lived memory of annihilation. This place where she cannot be known is one of catastrophic loneliness ... it is an area of deadness strangely infused with a yearning for life ... Death has possessed her in its impenetrable solitude. But life makes her desire to be known in that solitude ... [but] who will be the knower and who (and what) will be the known?
>
> (p. 4)

Grand has approached this question mindful of what she regards to be the lacunae inherent in the narration of traumatic experience, absences that denote trauma's presence. Grand has listened carefully to 'those human atrocities that can be neither seen nor heard in the survivor's testimony [and] actually retain their force through narrative absence' (2000, p. 24). She finds the traces of this force in the soma, where bodies bear witness to the unspeakable nature of events, containing, according to Grand, messages that defy their own translation. Grand regards these absences as experiences that will not simply yield to the fullness of symbolic representation, prompting her to note, 'We cannot conceive of the treatment of trauma as a path moving toward an emotionally integrated, linguistically encoded story in which bodily symptoms heal through their narration' (pp. 36–37). The persistence of affectivity signals a bodily registration which will not reside in conscious knowledge. Such memory, as Clough (2007, p. 6) has suggested, 'might better be understood not as unconscious memory so much as memory without consciousness and, therefore, incorporated memory, body memory, or cellular memory'.

I would further suggest that enactive memory phenomena in their bodily registration represent the essential force of trauma, which may only be experienced as event, rather than narration. Thus, what are often regarded to be gaps or lacunae in the verbal can be reconceptualized as experiences held in episodic memory systems which cannot be translated into language but convey the patients' reactions *as memory*.

Witnessing and symbolization

Within psychoanalysis, there is a constant expectation that traumatic experience will become symbolized. The assumption is seen both in Orange's goal of making meaning as well as in Grand's attention to the 'gaps' in coherent narrative. Conceptualizing 'absences' or 'gaps' presumes the expectation that trauma should or could become meaningful and that gaps represent a rupture in an expected narration, and, as Boris (1976, p. 150) has written, 'narration is spurious. It gives an order and meaning to experience which the experience is unlikely to possess'. Instead of assuming such memory can be translated into reflective, symbolic awareness, I will argue that its enactive quality calls for a response that does not require meaning-making or the telling of a story yet to be told. I share a perspective on working with trauma recently described by Bromberg (2009), who suggests an analytic focus 'on content creates a collusion between patient and analyst that leads to searching for what seems to be *hidden within the patient* and masks what is *absent between* them in the here-and-now' (p. 356), what he calls an 'affective awareness' of what is taking place between the two.

This perspective leads me to seek to broaden the notion of psychoanalytic witnessing. Analytic writing positions the analyst in the role of witness to the trauma experienced by the patient. Writers such as Orange, Poland and Grand, while representing theoretically diverse schools, all accord the witnessing function solely to the analyst. While not disagreeing with these authors, I propose expanding the notion of witnessing in two ways: First, I want to explore the patient's witnessing and the varieties of her capacity for witnessing within the analytic setting; I also want to open the idea of witnessing to encompass the relational event that occurs in the transference-countertransference matrix. This later event, I will suggest, is best met by a clinical position of 'being with' patients during the mutual living-out of traumatic memory phenomena. In order to approach that position, it will first be necessary to appreciate the ways in which speech creates performative action between analyst and patient.

Speech acts and the performative

The philosopher J. L. Austin (1962) conceived of uses of speech beyond its declarative function in the development of his speech act theory. Austin drew attention to the usages of language beyond the making of factual assertions to perform actions. In these instances, speech is itself considered a form of action, or, as Austin quipped, 'by saying something we *do* something' (p. 94). According to Petrey (1990), speech acts perform a collectivity that can be as small as two people (e.g. analysand and analyst) but performative speech can never be the unilateral act of a single individual. Thus the analyst saying to his analysand, 'Our time is up for today', is not merely making a factual assertion but performing an action within the therapeutic dyad. Speech act theory may be seen to underlie Schafer's (1976) conception of an action language, as well as Ogden's (1994) concept of interpretive action. Both Loewald (1978) and Greenberg (1996) have also observed that words do not substitute or hold back action, but are in themselves actions.

Within trauma studies, speech act theory is used both by Felman (1995) and Caruth (1996) to elaborate the performative aspects of testimony. The language of trauma, including its narrative gaps and absences, are regarded as a *doing*, in Austin's sense, which performs a truth or an actuality. Yet to think in theoretical terms about such absences is to regard the testimony of the witness as the individual's relation to an experience outside of understanding or narrative. Caruth (1996) has observed that trauma's mark eludes linguistic symbolic forms of articulation and meaning-making, and that the constitution of knowledge is 'a central problem of listening, of knowing, and of representing that emerges from the actual experience of . . . crisis' (p. 7). Crisis thus illuminates the limitations of its symbolic understanding. But while narrative may be absent, memory is not, and the fullness of traumatic impact remains. As Caruth puts it, 'The force of this experience would appear to arise precisely, in other words, in the collapse of its understanding' (1996, p. 7).

Similarly, Felman (1995) conceives of testimony as 'acts that cannot be construed as knowledge nor assimilated into full cognition, events in excess of our frames of reference' (p. 16). This is very much in concert with the theory of action and reproduction I am putting forward. Felman regards the testimony of the witness as representing 'a discursive *practice*' and the accomplishment of a speech act instead of the formulation of a statement. Felman writes,

> As a performative speech act, testimony in effect addresses what in history is action that exceeds any substantialized significance, and what in happenings is impact that dynamically explodes any conceptual reifications and any constative delimitations.
>
> (1995, p. 17)

Both Caruth and Felman speak to the experience of an individual's relation to an event that does not take the form of declarative recall. Their inclusion of non-symbolic experiencing informs an analytic approach to witnessing beyond the expectation of the creation of narrative, to focus on repeated 'modes of reaction' as they occur in the analytic relationship.

The transference as the scene of address

Non-psychoanalytic literature regards traumatic repetition as unmeaningful. Van der Kolk and van der Hart (1995) have written, 'Traumatic memory has no social component; it is not addressed to anybody, the patient does not respond to anybody; it is a solitary activity' (p. 163). By contrast, psychoanalytic approaches, since the time of *Studies on Hysteria* (1895), have emphasized an opposite approach.

Traumatic repetition is an inherently social event. It is not addressed to any particular person but it is addressed to an *other*. The other who can receive this experience is the analyst, who participates not as a blank slate, but whose affective presence within the analytic relationship creates the conditions for the mutual experiencing of that which exists outside speech. This communication occurs within performative and motoric dimensions of the transference-countertransference, conveying experience beyond the limits of human ability to grasp or imagine symbolically (Laub, 1991), but which allows patient and analyst to create an experience of witnessing.

If the patient's trauma seeks a witnessing through an encounter with the other, as I have suggested, then it is the transference that is the vehicle for that address. I propose that the transference acts as the scene of address for the simultaneous repetition and witnessing of traumatic memory in its performative and enactive form. The address does not occur between people, as one might say conventionally, rather it 'happens', as an action, within a scene.[1] It is lived, or performed, through what Bollas (2000, p. 112) has described as 'a showing by a relocating evocation'.

The purpose is not to transform the enactive into the reflective-verbal for, as Loewald (1965) observed, the notion that repetitions in the transference should be substituted with memories undermines Freud's understanding of action as a form of memory and memory as a form of action or repeating. Loewald encouraged analysts to not cling to 'narrow' distinctions between repeating and remembering, and instead makes a compelling argument for repetition within the transference:

> Reflection shows that precisely such transference repetitions, as well as similar kinds of repetition in the form of behavior or symptoms, have been described by Freud as reminiscences, i.e. as manifestations of unconscious memories. On the other hand, conscious remembering is a kind of repetition, a repetition in the mind. Repetition in the form of action or behavior and affect is a kind of remembering, albeit unconscious, and remembering as a conscious mental act is a kind of repetition. If one adheres, as psychoanalysis does, to the concept of unconscious memory, repetition and recollection can be understood in terms of each other, depending on whether we focus on the present act, in which case we speak of repeating, or on the past prototype, in which case we see recollection.
>
> (1965, p. 88)

As an enactive phenomenon, this happening is experienced as an *intensity* of traumatic activation, not yet as a content. The memory is the action, the affective reactivation of the body, rather than the content of an experience. This is similar to what Klein (1957, 1961) called 'memories in feelings' and may be thought of as experience's immanence in the immediacy of non-conscious affective exchange between patient and analyst.

Case vignette – Julie

Long before a narrative took shape in the material that Julie brought to our sessions, her body's staccato movements and her state of alert signalled the presence of a traumatic event. The way she scanned me, quickly and fearfully, took me by surprise. These looks were alternated with gasps of fear, in which she would draw in air as if about to be held underwater. Julie was terrified, and her body seemed to vibrate in a state of hyperaroused panic.

'Like this', Julie said as she lowered her head to her chest and pounded the air, fast and frantically. 'Like this, she would beat the wall, just like this'.

When it wasn't the wall, it was Julie's body that registered the rhythm of her psychotic mother's fists. Julie wondered how much of her mother's madness she held within herself, how much had been transferred by the fists and the screamed curses and the humiliation, how much madness had been put in her by the enemas that were forced on her, which we came to understand as violent and neglectful genital invasions. Julie wondered how much had been absorbed in the cells of her body. Her thoughts led to pounding the walls of her own office and as an accomplished senior attorney having to reassure her assistant that everything was fine, that she should go back to work.

Julie began hitting her own thighs. 'Like this', she repeated with tears now streaming down her face. As she hit herself in front of me, I told Julie that I saw what was happening. She looked into my face with an incredulous stare, as if she herself couldn't believe what was happening. During one unbelieving look, she said that she thought she could see my eyes tearing.

We began our work, meeting three times a week, first face-to-face, then after the better part of a year using the couch. My comments over the first years of the analysis mostly took the form of non-interpretive acknowledgements: that I was present, that I was seeing and hearing what she was experiencing. Whereas her passively depressed, 'vacant' father refused to acknowledge Julie's treatment at the hands of his wife, I saw and felt what she was feeling and communicated that in expression and tone. Julie's anguish and sorrow became my own, drawing on painful experiences from my past, which created receptive ground for the affective rather than the intellectualized grasp of her torment (Jacobs, 1991). I shared Julie's alarm and dread as I experienced a sense that something terrible was about to happen, and I accompanied her through unimaginable feelings of loneliness which put me in touch with a quality of loneliness from earlier in my own life. My attention to and immersion in Julie's feelings was an experience Bach (2006) has described as involving more than what is usually meant by empathy. The feelings were hers, but now experienced together, as her own, but now shared. Yet these moments were punctuated by Julie's loss of our psychic link. Terrified messages on my office answering machine attested to her fear that she could no longer continue the analysis. Leaving these messages, she told me, was her attempt to reconnect and regain the safety and attachment she found in our sessions. I made a point always to return these messages, and my short responses served to calm

Julie and repair the psychic rupture. As the analysis proceeded, she was able to internalize the feeling of our sessions and her need to phone my office answering machine abated.

In one session in the seventh year of analysis, she said,

> I remembered this after last morning's session on the way to the elevator, where I knew what was awaiting me. I knew when I woke up this morning that I would feel all the hunger and angst after our session – feel it again in the pit of my stomach. More, more screaming from inside me – a demand on the other side of my friend Jack's indifference and my sister's empty sadness. How to think of you in this hunger, you whose presence provokes it? I am thinking of the body I tried to bring into the room before I left the room, just laid down there before you, a body made of old stories and words but not it, not the rhythms of it. We are not in rhythm now because I have been away and the beats stopped beating. Still I left a body there; and then left there to find myself at the elevator, facing again being alone, so all alone at the elevator.

Moments such as these placed me on an analytic precipice. I was the intrusive, violent object to whom Julie offered herself up, laying herself bare emotionally with a mixture of fear and willingness. She offered herself to the analysis as she had offered her body to numerous men over her life, as she was afraid she had offered her body to her mother as a child. Yet at the same time, I was a distant and unreachable father, a man who Julie felt had abandoned her to her mother's madness, or 'discarded' her, to use her word. He was a man who Julie felt had the power to save her, but never did.

She continued,

> I am hungry and can't find enough to eat. Not enough to soothe. I do want to scream. I do. At you. I do. Hungry Daddy! I am. Something is repeating right now in the room but I don't know exactly what it is. Something is repeating. I am praying in the dark, kneeling beside the bed, prayers mixing with tears and blood. Can you hear my prayer? Can you hear me crying? I so need to know if you can hear me, if you are there to hear me. I am still praying, prayers mixed with blood and tears.

At the moment that Julie was searching for her passive father's response, I was present, witnessing the tears and pain of a memory without consciousness, enacted before my eyes. I began to notice within my countertransference an experience of confusion and sorrow, as something was repeated, not to be understood but to be experienced by me and us together.

Julie recalled masturbating at a very early age. Masturbation, she was willing to grant me, was indeed a form of self-soothing, but Julie was focused on its rhythmic quality. Motion and repetition were the forms of affect for what could not be cognitively understood or assimilated. Masturbation, like Julie's rocking in the sessions, was both the response and the event together, in a moment of experience. Julie looked up and said,

> If only I could sit in the session without speaking. If only I could rock and cry and not have to put words to it. I wanted to rock this morning. I wanted to rock, but I couldn't. I was embarrassed when you asked me about rocking yesterday. I was barely conscious of doing it but I was even less aware that you were noticing. I wish you had not asked and made it so hard for me to rock ever again. It hurts terribly to feel the loneliness from back then shot straight through all the years of my life. It's a terrible thing to feel it stronger for all the years I tried not to feel it. I feel so far away right now.

I said to Julie that I could feel that distance. There was a long pause in the session, and then she said,

> At first when you said that, I thought you meant that I do this thing where I push other people away from me and that was what I was doing to you. But then I thought, maybe he means he feels it too, that he's suffused with that feeling also, right now, and it made me feel very close to you.

Discussion

While the experience of enactive witnessing may be considered in terms of traditional psychoanalytic functions (i.e. containment, empathy or self-object experiencing), I have in mind an intersubjective concept that is based less on the notion of transforming an experience than transforming the patient's experience of an experience which I think occurred in Julie's shift from experiencing the analyst as together with her in the experience of distance rather than distant from her. Language cannot capture the implicit shadings and shifts of tone, expression or movement that occur in the flow of analytic work, much of it is too rapid and remains out of consciousness. My barely perceptible experiences in the countertransference – changes in my breathing, the tone of my voice and cadence of my words – represent just a portion of my reactions to Julie and her repetition of traumatic experience. Of course, my own somatosensory reactions were themselves shaped by a subjective history, called forth by intense moments of engagement with my patient. I would call this a receptivity to feeling and being emotionally acted upon. As the force of repetition came under the sway of the transference, it began to be transformed into a witnessing. Though it is difficult to convey in words this dimension of connection with another human being, it is the very specific quality of the presence of the analyst that creates the possibility for address where that possibility had been foreclosed. The way I was with Julie in moments of confusion, dread, terror and sorrow, with her and responding to her 'prayers mixed with blood and tears' created a different emphasis in her analysis, one not centred on the translation of trauma into meaning or understanding, but rather analytic participation in the rhythms of Julie's suffering, opening that suffering to a social dimension. Laub (1992b) writes,

> What ultimately matters in all processes of witnessing, spasmodic and continuous, conscious and unconscious, is not simply the information, the establishment of the facts, but the experience itself of living through testimony.
>
> (p. 85)

His insight is trenchant and made possible by the presence of an analytic other who lives through experience together with the patient (Grossmark, 2016), allowing her to reclaim more fully her position as a witness.

In the language of clinical psychoanalysis, this relational experience relies on what noted infant researcher Sander (1991) has defined as a recognition process, 'the specificity of another's being aware of what we experience being aware of within ourselves' (p. 9). This creates a dyadic form of self-organization for the individual. Lyons-Ruth (2000) extended Sander's conception of recognition process to non-conscious forms of coming to know one's self through the way one experiences being known. This is very close to my own (Reis, 2004) understanding of Winnicott's (1971) approach to the mirror role, where to see is to see oneself being seen by an *other* whose own experience creates the possibility for this seeing.

Trauma creates an imperative to communicate its impact but, without the appropriate encounter with an *other*, this imperative generally fails. Witnessing occurs in the encounter, but that encounter can never be guaranteed or predetermined. The address is thus not *in* the traumatic repetition but created in the encounter. Trauma's futurity may be a demand for future witnessing, but the creation of a witness occurs when another can turn that imperative into an address and thus a joint experience. What Bach (2006) has called a 'mutual living through' is central to a position of analytic witnessing that avoids premature interpretation of the clinical process.

The notion of speech acts arises from literary theory and the notion of enactive phenomena from a consideration of the motoric aspects of memory. These very different theories have in common a focus on action. In the analytic setting, this action necessarily involves the analyst, not as passive receiver of information, but as the addressee of traumatic testimony in its enactive form, filled with the force of traumatic experience. To the degree that the analyst's perception of the patient is also not a passive, receptive process but itself an active, motoric one, the analyst registers, feels and responds to enactive memory phenomena occurring in the consulting room at a somatic and affective level of engagement which may remain largely out of awareness. This is as true for the bodily enactive repetitions of the patient's 'modes of reaction' as it is for the speech acts that perform traumatic reproductions. Bridging the divide between these quite distinct linguistic and organic theories, Butler (2002) has observed that speaking itself is a bodily act and that there is no speech act without the body. She writes,

> The body is not 'outside' the speech act. At once the organ of speech, the very organic condition of speech, and the vehicle of speech, the body signifies the organic conditions for verbalization. So if there is no speech act without speech, and no speech without the organic, there is surely no speech act without the organic.
>
> (pp. 115–115)

Speech thus exceeds the conscious, cognitive intentions of its author. What speaks is the body, and it speaks of scandal and trauma (Felman, 2002). On the receiving end of these messages is the analyst, to whose body the spoken act is directed as an address so full of affective experience it exceeds its own linguistic form.

While I have maintained that the clinical aim of analytic witnessing is not to symbolize enactive memory phenomena or create coherent narrative, it would be wrong to suggest that through the analysis, Julie did not come to know more about the early events in her life. Julie changed dramatically. She acknowledged openly a wish to love and be loved, as she had never done before, and her relationships deepened as she no longer took refuge in working. 'Something opened', she said, and she was able to feel how much she wanted others in her life. She was astonished to learn that she was in contact with others and that they were in contact with her: 'I can hear people, and I can tell they're hearing me'. Colleagues began asking for her incisive legal opinions, and now she heard their admiration. Julie was, in so many ways, better as a result of the analysis, but she was not without her experience of trauma. Analysis had not put an end to Julie's experience of enactive memory phenomena, nor had it produced a neat narrative of previously unknown experience. What it did do, however, was provide Julie with an experience of 'being with' (Reis, 2018) an *other*, which featured response in the moment of experienced crisis. It was not knowing more about the past that led to Julie being able to hear others and expect that they would hear her. What led to Julie's ability to contact others and be contacted by them was an intersubjective experience at the limits of understanding.

Note

1 By this I mean to imply that it is both analyst and patient who witness what is reproduced in the space of the therapeutic relationship, as neither is solely accorded the role of witness to the other's separate experience.

References

Austin, J.L. (1962). *How to Do Things with Words*. Cambridge, MA: Harvard University Press.

Bach, S. (2006). *Getting from Here to There*. Hillsdale: Analytic Press.

Bollas, C. (2000). *Hysteria*. New York: Routledge.
Boris, H.N. (1976). 'On Hope: Its Nature and Psychotherapy.' *International Journal of Psycho-Analysis*, 3: 139–150.
Boston Change Process Study Group. (2013). 'Enactment and the Emergence of New Relational Organization.' *Journal of the American Psychoanalytic Association*, 61(4), 727–749.
Breuer, J. & Freud, S. (1893). 'On the Psychical Mechanism of Hysterical Phenomenon: A Preliminary Communication.' *S.E.* 2: 3–17.
Bromberg, P.M. (2009). 'Truth, Human Relatedness and the Analytic Process.' *International Journal of Psychoanalysis*, 90: 347–361.
Bromberg, P.M. (2011a). *The Shadow of the Tsunami: And the Growth of the Relational Mind*. New York: Routledge.
Bromberg, P.M. (2011b). *Awakening the Dreamer: Clinical Journeys*. New York: Routledge.
Bruner, J.S., Oliver, R.R. & Greenfield, P.M. (1966). *Studies in Cognitive Growth*. New York: Wiley.
Bucci, W. (1997). *Psychoanalysis and Cognitive Science: A Multiple Code Theory*. New York: The Guilford Press.
Butler, J. (2002). 'Afterword.' In: S. Felman (Ed.) *The Scandal of the Speaking Body*. Stanford: Stanford University Press, pp. 113–123.
Caruth, C. (1996). *Unclaimed Experience: Trauma, Narrative, and History*. Baltimore: Johns Hopkins University Press.
Chefetz, R.A. & Bromberg, P.M. (2004). 'Talking with "Me" and "Not-Me": A Dialogue.' *Contemporary Psychoanalysis*, 40(3): 409–464.
Clough, P.T. (2007). 'Introduction.' In: P.T. Clough & J. Halley (Eds.) *The Affective Turn*. Durham: Duke University Press, pp. 1–33.
Clyman, R.B. (1991). 'The Procedural Organization of Emotions: A Contribution from Cognitive Science to the Psychoanalytic Theory of Therapeutic Action.' *Journal of the American Psychoanalytic Association*, 39S: 349–382.
Felman, S. (1995). 'Education and Crisis, or the Vicissitudes of Teaching.' In: C. Caruth (Ed.) *Trauma: Explorations in Memory*. Baltimore: Johns Hopkins University Press, pp. 13–60.
Felman, S. (2002). *The Scandal of the Speaking Body*. Stanford: Stanford University Press.
Freud, S. (1895a). 'Project for a Scientific Psychology.' *S.E.*, Vol. 1, London: Hogarth Press, pp. 295–397.
Freud, S. (1895b). 'The Psychotherapy of Hysteria.' *S.E.*, Vol. 2, London: Hogarth Press, pp. 253–305.
Freud, S. (1900). 'The Interpretation of Dreams.' *S.E.*, Vols. 4–5, London: Hogarth Press.
Freud, S. (1914). 'Remembering, Repeating, and Working Through.' *S.E.*, Vol. 12, London: Hogarth Press, pp. 145–156.
Freud, S. (1917). 'Introductory Lectures on Psychoanalysis.' *S.E.*, Vol. 16, London: Hogarth Press, pp. 241–463.
Freud, S. (1925). 'Mystic Writing Pad.' *S.E.*, Vol. 19, London: Hogarth Press, pp. 225–232.
Freud, S. (1937). 'Analysis Terminable and Interminable.' *S.E.*, Vol. 23, London: Hogarth Press, pp. 216–253.
Grand, S. (2000). *The Reproduction of Evil*. Hillsdale: Analytic Press.
Greenberg, J. (1996). 'Psychoanalytic Words and Psychoanalytic Acts – A Brief History.' *Contemporary Psychoanalysis*, 32: 195–213.

Grossmark, R. (2016). 'Psychoanalytic Companioning.' *Psychoanalytic Dialogues*, 26(6): 698–712.

Grossmark, R. (2018). *The Unobtrusive Relational Analyst: Explorations in Psychoanalytic Companioning*. New York: Routledge.

Jacobs, T. (1991). 'The Inner Experience of the Analyst: Their Contributions to the Analytic Process.' *International Journal of Psychoanalysis*, 74: 7–14.

Klein, M. (1957). 'Envy and Gratitude.' In: *The Writings of Melanie Klein*, Vol. 3. London: Hogarth, 1975, pp. 176–235.

Klein, M. (1961). 'Narrative of Child Analysis.' In: *The Writings of Melanie Klein*, Vol. 4: London: Hogarth, 1975.

Laub, D. (1991). 'Truth and Testimony: The Process and the Struggle.' In: C. Caruth (Ed.) *Trauma: Explorations in Memory*. Baltimore: Johns Hopkins, University Press, pp. 61–75.

Laub, D. (1992a). 'Bearing Witness: Or the Vicissitudes of Listening.' In: S. Felman & D. Laub (Eds.) *Testimony: Crises of Witnessing in Literature, Psychoanalysis, and History*. New York: Routledge, pp. 57–74.

Laub, D. (1992b). 'An Event Without a Witness: Truth, Testimony and Survival.' In: S. Felman & D. Laub (Eds.) *Testimony: Crises of Witnessing in Literature, Psychoanalysis, and History*. New York: Routledge, pp. 75–92.

Loewald, H.W. (1965). 'Some Considerations on Repetition and Repetition Compulsion.' In: *The Essential Loewald: Collected Papers and Monographs*. Hagerstown: University Publishing Group, pp. 87–101.

Loewald, H.W. (1976). 'Perspectives on Memory.' In: *The Essential Loewald: Collected Papers and Monographs*. Hagerstown: University Publishing Group, pp. 148–173.

Loewald, H.W. (1978). 'Primary Process, Secondary Process and Language.' In: *The Essential Loewald: Collected Papers and Monographs*. Hagerstown: University Publishing Group, pp. 87–101.

Lyons-Ruth, K. (1998). 'Implicit Relational Knowing: Its Role in Development and Psychoanalytic Treatment.' *Infant Mental Health Journal*, 19: 282–289.

Lyons-Ruth, K. (2000). 'I Sense That You Sense That I Sense : Sander's Recognition Process and the Specificity of Relational Moves in the Psychotherapeutic Setting.' *Infant Mental Health Journal*, 21: 85–98.

Nahum, J. (2017). 'What Is Enactment What Is Dissociation?' *Psychoanalytic Dialogues*, 27(5): 621–629.

Ogden, T.H. (1989). *The Primitive Edge of Experience*. Northvale: Jason Aronson.

Ogden, T.H. (1994). 'The Concept of Interpretive Action.' *Psychoanalytic Quarterly*, 63: 219–245.

Orange, D. (1995). *Emotional Understanding: Studies in Psychoanalytic Epistemology*. New York: The Guilford Press.

Petrey, S. (1990). *Speech Acts and Literary Theory*. New York: Routledge.

Poland, W. (2000). 'The Analyst's Witnessing and Otherness.' *Journal of the American Psychoanalytic Association*, 48: 17–34.

Reis, B. (2004). 'You Are Requested to Close the Eyes.' *Psychoanalytic Dialogues*, 14: 349–371.

Reis, B. (2009a). 'Performative and Enactive Features of Psychoanalytic Witnessing: The Transference as the Scene of Address.' *International Review of Psycho-Analysis*, 90(6): 1359–1372.

Reis, B. (2009b). 'We: Commentary on Papers by Trevarthen, Ammaniti & Trentini, and Gallese.' *Psychoanalytic Dialogues*, 19(5): 565–579.

Reis, B. (2010). 'Enactive Fields: An Approach to Interaction in the Kleinian-Bionian Model: Commentary on Paper by Lawrence J. Brown.' *Psychoanalytic Dialogues*, 20(6): 695–703.
Reis, B. (2018). 'Being-with: From Infancy Through Philosophy to Psychoanalysis.' In: C. Bonovitz & A. Harlem (Eds.) *Developmental Perspectives in Child Psychoanalysis and Psychotherapy*. New York: Routledge, pp. 13–26.
Sander, L. (1991). 'Recognition Process: Specificity and Organization in Early Human Development.' Paper presented at University of Massachusetts conference on 'The psychic life of the infant'.
Schafer, R. (1976). *A New Language for Psychoanalysis*. New Haven: Yale University Press.
Stern, D.B. (2010). *Partners in Thought*. New York: Routledge.
Stern, D.N., Sander, L., Nahum, J., Harrison, A., Lyons-Ruth, K., Morgan, A., Bruschweiler-Stern, N. & Tronick, E.Z. (1998). 'Non-Interpretive Mechanisms in Psychoanalytic Therapy: The "Something More" Than Interpretation.' *International Review of Psycho-Analysis*, 79: 903–921.
Van der Kolk, B.A. & van der Hart, O. (1995). 'The Intrusive Past: The Flexibility of Memory and the Engraving of Trauma.' In: C. Caruth (Ed.) *Trauma: Explorations in Memory*. Baltimore: Johns Hopkins Press, pp. 158–182.
Winnicott, D.W. (1971). 'Mirror Role of Mother and Family in Child Development.' In: D. Winnicott (Ed.) *Playing and Reality*. London: Tavistock Publications, pp. 111–118.

Chapter 6

Silence and quiet
A phenomenology of wordlessness

In a curious development, analysts from every school appear to be in agreement that the patient's silence in the session should no longer merely be regarded as a resistance to free association and the analyst's silence no longer be solely regarded as the provision of optimal anxiety, as they were initially conceived (see Calogeras, 1967 for a historical overview). As noted in a panel report (Wheeler Vega, 2013) from the recent meetings of the American Psychoanalytic Association, an American relational, a British Kleinian, American classical and South American child and adolescent analyst were all in agreement that silence carried a wide range of possible functions and meanings, was in itself communicative, and not be to considered opposed to speech. Should we be worried? These are analytic schools that cannot agree on almost any facet of psychoanalysis, and yet we find robust agreement when it comes to the issue of silence. Perhaps we can understand this by conjecturing that silence affords a certain freedom to analysts, to dwell in a space that affords room for thinking over the application of a prescribed method.

I would like to begin my examination of this subject by making a distinction: between silence and quiet. In psychoanalysis, silence is often thought of as the absence of speaking, conceptualized with reference to the analyst's technique or what is repressed or withheld by the patient. I would say quiet is a more expansive term, associated with lived experience in the psychoanalytic relationship between patient and analyst – i.e. thoughtfulness. Quiet is an experience that is embedded in the *practice* of psychoanalysis. Practice differs from technique in that it is an engagement in the interaction that takes prominence over the application of a method. I should add that these terms, silence and quiet, have been used interchangeably in psychoanalytic literature, so by separating them, I intend to illustrate the varieties of experience between the silent and quiet analytic pair.

To speak of silence is to speak of issues of technique (Arlow, 1961; Calogeras, 1967). The silence of the analyst has been considered a technical parameter, the silence of the patient, a technical issue to be addressed, though as Salberg (2012) has observed, this division has not been followed neatly. I would say that silence in the psychoanalytic set-up can only be thought of as the absence of speech, given the original parameters of the talking cure. Silence is muteness, a refusal to speak when expected. This absence of sound is a condition that has conventionally been understood either to inhibit or facilitate the psychoanalytic process, depending upon whether it is performed by patient or analyst. Wedded in this way to speech, silence is inseparable from considerations of method and methodology. It is thus bound to matters of control and the rule-bound reproduction of a method – the *psychoanalytic* method.

Interpersonally, silence in the psychoanalytic set-up is associated with terms such as withdrawal and withholding. The patient withdraws into silence. The analyst withholds his reactions. Retreat, refusal, and detachment are the forms through which silence is always wedded. Withdrawing and withholding are by definition positions that draw the individual back into him or herself and out of the relationship. Such mute, narcissistic retreats reveal the solitary nature of silence. One is silent alone. Silence renders one out of contact, out of communication. But is this always a problem? And shouldn't there be a place in our theory for silent withdrawal? Winnicott (1963) reminds us that

> there is something we must allow for in our work, the patient's non-communicating as a positive contribution . . . We must ask ourselves, does our technique allow for the patient to communicate that he or she is not communicating? For this to happen we as analysts must be ready for the signal: 'I am not communicating,' and be able to distinguish it from the distress signal associated with a failure of communication.
>
> (p. 188)

Here, as so often, Winnicott is providing balance by allowing for the psychoanalytic space of non-communication to be one of positive solitude and privacy, and for the action of withdrawal to serve as a basis for what he calls a 'capacity for withdrawal', which underlies an ability for absorption in a task.

By contrast, quiet may be the absence of words, but it is not necessarily solitary. Where silence signals withdrawal and withholding, quiet marks a 'with-ness' between patient and analyst. Suzanne Little (2015) notes the dual character of quiet when she writes,

> Quiet is the background of being. It speaks to an area of aliveness prior to doing and relating that is more existential than interactional, and is a precondition for learning to be with what Winnicott (1988) refers to as 'essential aloneness.' Quiet is also a way of being with a patient, of being attuned to the developmental frequencies of relatedness, the degrees of closeness and apartness, which reverberate in that felicitous phrase, 'living an experience together.'

A child may be quiet, on the other side of the room from its mother and be with her, that is to say, even alone, in the presence of an *other*, as the mother is with her child (Winnicott, 1958). It is not a withdrawal so much as it is a togetherness without words. They may be engaged with one another through eye contact or involved in their own pursuits, but they are with each other in a way that does not evoke words like retreat, refusal or detachment. Michael Balint (1968) provides an illustration of this in the report of a treatment that accords with the emphasis the British Independents put on the development of the self, free from impingement by others. The paradigm is one of developmental growth in the analytic context that results in the patient finding something entirely his or herself within the space of the treatment. Balint writes of one patient who after being in analysis for two years,

> remained silent, right from the start of the session for more than thirty minutes; the analyst accepted it and, realizing what was possibly happening, waited without any attempt whatever at interfering, in fact, he did not even feel uncomfortable or under pressure to do something . . . the silence was eventually broken by the patient starting to sob, relieved, and soon after he was about to speak. He told his analyst that at long last he was able to reach himself; ever since childhood he had never been left alone, there had always been someone telling him what to do. Some sessions later he reported that during the silence he had all sorts of associations but rejected each of them as irrelevant, as nothing but an annoying superficial nuisance.
>
> (p. 142)

Quieting is an active verb. When a mother attempts to soothe her overly aroused child she says 'shh'. She tries not to silence the child, but to calm her, to quiet her. Here we have the definition of quiet as the ability to be put at rest rather than silenced. An analyst calms her patient by speaking quietly, perhaps reassuringly, and the patient finds him or herself taking deeper breaths, feeling less overwhelmed. Most often, this occurs without conscious awareness, allowing the dyad to settle into a quieter place. Perhaps they go on to discuss what had upset the patient, but now they can do so without feeling danger or being overly alert.

When analysts are quiet perhaps they are engaged in reverie. Not a retreat or detachment, but a place where they can explore the depths of unconscious linkage. There is no technique to this dream space, only the ability to dream and associate fluidly. The patient may be speaking during the analyst's reverie, or he or she may not. But the feeling of an engaged, quiet analyst is completely different from that of a technically silent one. Here is an example of a silent patient and a quiet analyst. Again, it was Winnicott (1968) who advised the analyst not to seek understanding, or exercise the intellectual skills they have acquired in the course of being analysts. With a silent patient, Winnicott takes great care to not 'put words in his mouth', as the saying goes:

> [A] rather silent patient tells the analyst, in response to a question, a good deal about one of his main interests, which has to do with shooting pigeons and the organization of this kind of sport. It is extremely tempting for the

analyst at this point to use this material, which is more than he often gets in two or three weeks, and undoubtedly he could talk about the killing of all the unborn babies, the patient being an only child, and he could talk about the unconscious destructive fantasies in the mother, the patient's mother having been a depressive case and having committed suicide. What the analyst knew, however, was that the whole material came from a question and that it would not have come if the analyst had not invited the material, perhaps simply out of feeling that he was getting out of touch with the patient. The material therefore was not material for interpretation and the analyst had to hold back all that he could imagine in regard to the symbolic meaning of the activity which the patient was describing. After a while the analysis settled back into being a silent one and it is the patient's silence which contains the essential communication. The clues to this silence are only slowly emerging and there is nothing directly that this analyst can do to make the patient talk.

(p. 210)

In this quotation, I think we can see nicely how silence and quiet may be thought of as not opposed to each other, but in a dialectical relationship so that the analyst's quiet is a foreground phenomenon, with the potential for his silence (as an artefact of his analytic method and informing the creation of quiet). The patient is allowed his silent withdrawal and Winnicott understands this as 'the essential communication'. To quote Thomas Ogden (1999),

> To privilege speaking over silence, disclosure over privacy, communicating over not-communicating, seems as unanalytic as it would be to privilege the positive transference over the negative transference, gratitude over envy, love over hate, the depressive mode of generating experience over the paranoid-schizoid and autistic contiguous modes.
>
> (p. 123)

In the quotation from Winnicott, one can also appreciate the emphasis he places on what comes from the patient, rather than what comes from involvement with or invitation from the analyst. Balint (1968) also highly valued this aspect of silence and speech in his belief that within the regressive context of psychoanalytical treatment the patient may contact parts of their own mind that he called the 'area of creation' (p. 176). Rather than considering the patient's silence simply as resistance – i.e. a running away from something – he saw the opportunity for the patient to move towards something by being in silence. That which the patient would encounter or discover would be something all his own, arrived at through an act of creation.

The analyst also needs to be quiet inside, to listen to what is happening, to what gets set off inside him when sitting with his patient. Speech tends to dispel this kind of inner quiet. This is what led the British Independent analyst Michael Parsons to critique relational approaches as 'internally rather busy' (2009, p. 264). Parsons finds an approach in which the analyst is busy disclosing their own internal process, asking patients about their reactions to the analyst and their interventions and about what may be going on between them as an impediment to a kind of deep listening to what is going on inside the analyst. Parsons writes, 'In the analyst's inner world, just as with the patient, the responses which matter most are those that need time and space to surface out of the unconscious. I think we need to listen slowly' (ibid.).

The context of listening slowly is one factor that makes the psychoanalytic conversation different from ordinary social conversation. One cannot but live this kind of slow listening as a 'being with' the patient (Reis, 2009, 2018). Slow listening depends on a quiet that is not silence. The quiet analyst may be without words for some time before commenting on an experience. They may live through quite a lot with their patient and not necessarily seek to symbolize or make understandable after the fact what has transpired between them. For the analyst, as for the patient, there are sorts of quiet too, those which occur within the analytic dialogue and between sessions. Gabbard (2012, p. 586) writes,

> In the ebb and flow of the analytic dialogue, we are at times an analytic couple and at times a separate entity that the patient cannot fully know. Neither can the analyst fully know the patient. We discover parts of the self in the interplay with the patient while finding other aspects of who we are in the rich silences between sessions, as we think about the patient who has just left and the patient who has not yet arrived. We live and breathe in the context of *vínculos* even if a crisp definition escapes our grasp. It is our fate to live simultaneously in the present with the external patient who lies before us as well as in the past with the ghosts, ancestors, and demons that haunt the nether-regions of our *unconscious*.

In the session, the quiet patient may be taking repose. He may have found an area of life where speech is not demanded of him. It is ironic that in the context of the talking cure, he finds the oasis of quiet which allows peace and reflection, a space to be alone with his analyst. Sitting quietly with another person over time is one of the most intimate acts available to us as people. As Searles (1979, p. 27) wrote, an experience of this sort need not necessarily be felt as 'a gulf, a void, but may be a tangibly richer communion than any words could constitute'.

The paradoxical nature of reverie involves accessing dimensions of intersubjective experience that arrive in solitary and personal forms. Transcending dichotomous conceptualizations of a one-person vs. two-person psychology, sitting quietly with another person is at once a sharing of aloneness with another in addition to a deep unconscious connection. Elsewhere (Reis, 2018), I have employed the work of the philosopher Jean-Luc Nancy (1993) to describe this form of non-mediated, non-dialectical relation of encounter. His use of the French word 'partager', meaning both sharing and dividing, captures the idea I have that a psychoanalytic connection lies in our mutual separation and that what most holds us in common is this separating-connecting. Quiet is the sound made by this condition.

References

Arlow, J.A. (1961). 'Silence and the Theory of Technique.' *Journal of the American Psychoanalytic Association*, 9: 44–55.
Balint, M. (1968). *The Basic Fault*. New York: Brunner Mazel.
Calogeras, R.C. (1967). 'Silence as a Technical Parameter in Psycho-Analysis.' *International Journal of Psycho-Analysis*, 48: 536–558.
Gabbard, G.O. (2012). 'Deconstructing Vínculo.' *Psychoanalytic Quarterly*, 81(3): 579–587.
Little, S. (2015). 'Between Silence and Words: The Therapeutic Dimension of Quiet.' *Contemporary Psychoanalysis*, 51(1): 31–50.
Nancy, J.L. (1993). *The Experience of Freedom*. Redwood City, CA: Stanford University Press.
Ogden, T. (1999). *Reverie and Interpretation: Sensing Something Human*. London: Karnac Books.
Parsons, M. (2009). 'Reply to Commentaries.' *Psychoanalytic Dialogues*, 19: 259–266.
Reis, B. (2009). 'Performative and Enactive Features of Psychoanalytic Witnessing: The Transference as the Scene of Address.' *International Journal of Psycho-Analysis*, 90(6): 1359–1372.
Reis, B. (2018). 'Being-with: From Infancy Through Philosophy to Psychoanalysis.' In: C. Bonovitz & A. Harlem (Eds.) *Developmental Perspectives in Child Psychoanalysis and Psychotherapy*. New York: Routledge, pp. 13–26.
Salberg, J. (2012). 'Silence: Now More Than Ever: Contemporary Relational and Freudian Perspectives.' *Division/Rev.*, 6: 18.
Searles, H. (1979). *The Non-human Environment in Normal Development and in Schizophrenia*. New York: International Universities Press.
Wheeler Vega, J.A. (2013). 'Silence, Now.' *Journal of the American Psychoanalytic Association*, 61(6): 1211–1225.
Winnicott, D.W. (1958). 'The Capacity to Be Alone.' In: D.W. Winnicott (Ed.) *The Maturational Processes and the Facilitating Environment*. New York: International Universities Press, 1965, pp. 29–36.
Winnicott, D.W. (1963). 'Communicating and Not Communicating Leading to a Study of Certain Opposites.' In: D.W. Winnicott (Ed.) *The Maturational Process and the Facilitating Environment*. New York: International Universities Press, 1965, pp. 179–192.
Winnicott, D.W. (1968). 'Interpretation in Psycho-Analysis.' In: C. Winnicott, R. Shepherd & M. Davis (Eds.) *Psycho-Analytic Explorations*. Cambridge, MA: Harvard University Press, 1989, pp. 207–212.
Winnicott, D.W. (1988). 'A Primary State of Being: Pre-Primitive Stages.' In *Human Nature*. Philadelphia, PA: Brunner-Mazel, pp. 131–134.

Chapter 7

Form and content

> I am not among the hardhats dismissive of identifiable content, on the contrary, but poetry that does not really take language seriously into account – make that foremost: its texture, smell, shape, strength, options, registers, tonalities, etymologies, as well as its wide margins of error; how loudly it can play, how softly, and so forth; poetry that does not take formal acts into account: those weird, elusive organizing openings that the material presents, whether form is an extension of content or content is an extension of form, without obtaining to some sense of form – I cannot distinguish it from prose to any credible degree necessitating it being 'a poem.' Do I contradict myself? Very well then I contradict myself. It's a poem if I say it is. In his notebooks Oppen declared in his declarative way, 'Form is what makes the thing graspable so you can know what is being said and why it was said and how it weighs. Until it takes form you haven't written it.
>
> C.D. Wright (2016, p. 88)

Ever since Freud advanced the Kantian position, popular in nineteenth-century German intellectual thought, that we have no direct access to things-in-themselves and only experience 'thing presentations' that need to be transformed into 'word presentations' in order to be known; analysts have built their metapsychologies around this notion. Creating symbols out of emotional experience without form has been tied by analysts of different schools to the development of mind, to the digestion and processing of early traumatic experience and to the birth of a psychological subject. As much of this book does not concentrate on words, it remains for me to express what I feel to be important with regard to the issue of words and their function in psychoanalysis – i.e. here I shall revisit that 'old business about form and content', as Wright (ibid.) put it.

Currently in psychoanalysis, there remains a tremendous emphasis on the symbolization of experience. Analysts attempt to find form in unrepresented states (Civitarese, 2013) through a process of analytic figurability. But what are these not-yet experiences before they reach form and in what state might they persist in the unconscious? If, as with a poem, we can only grasp an experience that is given form, how do we conceptualize some of the contents of the unconscious that are understood to exist over time, and what happens to an original experience when it is given form? Sometimes, these psychoanalytic matters resemble medieval debates regarding how many angels could dance on the head of a pin – which is to say that the topic is complex, that many of the answers are ultimately unknowable and that the conversation tends towards the highly theoretical. It is not the answers to these questions that I feel to be important as much as the interrogation of these themes and the resulting implications for analytic technique. There are for instance analysts (LaFarge, 2014) who maintain that the contents of the unconscious can be discovered or uncovered in forms which predate the analysis. And there are others who maintain that the contents of the unconscious are constructed or co-constructed in the intersubjective relation of analysand and analyst (Levine, 2013). Both are correct, of course, but often at different times. It is surprising how much this issue can divide analysts into camps and with differing techniques and goals. Words do different kinds of conceptual work in each of these psychoanalytic models.

While the issue of representation has claimed centre stage, one must be mindful of the implications of believing a piece of unrepresented unconscious experience can be transformed into a knowable piece of conscious experience. Humans have an innate wish for meaning and apply that constructive wish to the mundane, the inchoate, and the mysterious. It chafes at us that there are things we cannot ever know, and so, sometimes, we pretend to know. In taking an all too confident approach to the meaning of unrepresented unconscious content, it is possible to defensively put the ambiguities and terrors of unconscious life to one side – e.g. transform our notion of unconscious life to life that is simply *not yet* conscious. But such content is not conscious content in another place; it is not disguised content, nor is it material awaiting an isomorphic translation. It is made of different stuff and is difficult to conceptualize. If it is unrepresented, then it occupies no one place, form or time in a particular narrative. It is the uncanny, the foreign; it disrupts rather than brings closure, knowledge or continuity.

While analysts have explored the relation of form and content in numerous ways, I will highlight some of the approaches that have resonated with me. Bollas (2011) has considered the dichotomy between form and content to be functional in the demand it makes on the individual to engage in thinking, either within oneself or with another. Nettleton (2017, p. 44) notes that for Bollas, the unconscious form of an experience often needs to be transformed 'into a form that will render it thinkable, moving it from the presentational to the representational so that it can be mediated by consciousness'. It is of particular interest that in Bollas's scheme, it is the moving itself that helps to contain the experience within words and thoughts, even if losing some of the experience is part of this moving and may be essential to the moving. Moving itself is a creative process that will shape the words that result, as well as allowing the effects of unconscious experience to reach consciousness.

On this issue, Bollas (2011) himself writes,

> Talking aims to transform the real into the symbolic, and even if this fails to represent the presentations of the experience it *adheres* to the experience and carries its after-effect in verbal form. Even if we do not turn to actual others we may have an internal dialogue about the recent encounter in which memory functions as a dynamic container for the after-effects of the real.
>
> (p. 242, my italics)

For Bollas, something of the experience is captured, and the rest may fall outside of what can be named or what can be withstood. Indeed, the rest may play in contrapuntal fashion, creating a ground for conscious elaboration that resists conscious understanding itself. The goal is phenomenological rather than epistemic. As Bollas (1993 saw it, the process is meant 'not to print out unconscious meaning but to discover objects that conjugate into meaning-laden experience' (p. 65).

In this way, the symbol, for Bollas, as for the philosopher Suzanne Langer (1957), carries the thinker's way of thinking with regard to the object. Langer (1957) wrote,

> Symbols are not proxy for their objects, but are vehicles for the conception of objects. To conceive a thing or a situation is not the same thing as to 'react toward it' overtly, or to be aware of its presence. In talking about things we have conceptions of them, not the things themselves; and it is the conceptions, not the things, that symbols directly 'mean'.
>
> (Langer, 1957, pp. 60–61)

A symbol is paired for an individual with a conception that fits an object or experience. Going beyond referring to an object in absentia, humans also use symbols to communicate states of mind with regard to objects and experience. G. H. Mead (1934) wrote,

> It involves not only communication in the sense in which birds and animals communicate with each other, but also an arousal in the individual himself of the response he is calling out in the other individual, a taking of the role of the other, a tendency to act as the other person acts.
>
> (Mead, 1934, p. 73)

Bollas (1993 p. 62) further explored the relationship between form and content by discussing the ways in which one may be *informed* by others:

> I can talk to my analyst about my father, but what happens over time is that he will know him less through the precise contents of the associations than

through some intriguing effect upon himself which gathers into his inner experiencing something of the nature of what I hold within myself.

This conception rests upon Bollas's idea of a receptive unconscious, the permeability of which allows for the reception of unconsciously transmitted communications from the other.

One can see how the process Nettleton (2017) described of transforming unconscious experience, moving it from the presentational to the representational (content to form) is not a simple matter of translation into words. The relation of what is considered content to what is considered form is quite complex: In some instances, form reflects content, and in other instances, it adheres to the unconscious experience and reflects its after-effects. Sometimes form can *inform* through repeated exposures to a person, thus constituting a content in itself which exists beyond the words that have been exchanged and what is possible to say. All of which is to say that it is difficult to speak of words in and of themselves in psychoanalysis. In order to take language seriously, one must do as C. D. Wright suggested at the beginning of this chapter, appreciate the texture, sound, shape, etc. One must also take into account that language and words in psychoanalysis are spoken and that it is speech that exists at the centre of our enterprise, and speech has its own relation to words.

Some of the most exciting psychoanalytic work on speech surprisingly comes from contemporary French psychoanalysis. I say surprisingly because of the outsized influence Lacanian theory has exerted over French approaches for decades. But analysts such as Aulagnier, whose work Miller (2015) has described as constituting a radical departure from Lacan, both conceptually and clinically, return both the body and affect to the centre of psychoanalytic drive theory. In the work of Green (1999), one also sees via the hallucinatory transformation of thing representations in the preconscious the meeting of drive, word and affect. For these and other French theorists, one doesn't speak of words without also speaking of affects and the body. As in the work of Bollas, it is the effect words may have that constitutes their analytic message.

In an important piece on listening to the patient's speech, Dominique Clerc (2007) wrote that once one takes

> into account that in any discourse by the patient [there is a] hallucinogenic force of words, which are due to their instinctual charge, [this] leads to the abandonment of a mode of translation which would rely only on the purely symbolic order of language and [instead] give its full emphasis to the *impression* left by words.
>
> (2007, p. 23, my italics)

Clerc returns to Freud, whose early attention to the patient's speech comprised listening to its breaks and shifts, and whose later attention focused on listening involving the action of the analyst 'where the activity of construction is posited as the equivalent of a delirium' (Clerc, 2007, p. 23). Clerc's emphasis is on listening to the unique speech of one's patient and on the effect their words have on the analyst, the one who hears them in the unique context of a psychoanalysis:

> Each cure thus constitutes a particular experience, merely because the deployment it offers to the word is singular each time, and summons the particular attention of the one who proposes to hear it . . . In this sense the 'cure de parole' is also 'cure d'ecoute'.
>
> (Clerc, 2007, p. 1)

In this conception, words are deployed and create effects because the analytic setting makes possible the presence of an *other* whose 'particular attention' will be 'summoned' by them (Gentile, 2016). Words are transmitted in speech, which itself has a special quality, and thus it is the analyst's listening that registers their special impressions.

In North America, analysts have been guided for decades by a prohibition against action, which has been split off from speech as the preferred mode of analytic interaction. Thus for years, speech became about the patient's disembodied words, a text to be deciphered by another disembodied mind, rationally, and free from the intrusion of affect. More recently, as discussed in Chapter 5, North American analysts (e.g. Greenberg, 1996) have begun to embrace the fact that words perform an action within psychoanalysis (i.e. they 'do things') and that action also may be a form of eloquent speech (Grossmark, 2018).

For Clerc, as for the other French theorists mentioned earlier, words hold the hallucinogenic force of the instinctual charge they represent. They contain 'magical power' (Freud, 1917) that has suffered from being confined to the limitations of speech and listening, and the analyst's job is to re-find in them the charge they possess. Revisiting Freud's (1926) conversation with an imagined interlocutor who curiously questions how an analysis between patient and analyst works, we see that 'there is nothing between them but this: they speak to each other'. Clerc described the questioner as astonished, offended and, perhaps, slightly condescending, suggesting such a practice is akin to magic. Freud replied that the word does indeed conceal a magic power which belongs to its very origin. The word, he said, is nothing less than the substitute for the act. Words, then, are magical actions which underpin the cure through speaking. But words have lost the marvelous character of their origin because of the detours that speech and listening have created. It is an idea such as this one that led Baranger and Baranger (2008, p. 823) to suggest that perhaps

> the problem of the specific action of the word has . . . been formulated backwards: it is not a question of trying to know how words reach the unconscious contents of the analytic situation but why and how words have lost their original power to reach deeply into internal life, a power that they retain in certain circumstances (poetry, song, incantations, a leader's discourse, etc.).

Re-finding the magical action of words brings form and content together again in a complex manner. The talking cure is rooted not only in the magic contained in words that are spoken but also in the presence of a listener whose particular attention is summoned by them. This understanding allows me to link Clerc's notion of listening to the speech of the patient, with the clinical phenomena I am addressing in this book: the monsters, dreams and madness which emerge in the consulting room. The connection begins with silence, for just as I emphasized a central role for silence in the analytic space (see Chapter 6), Clerc also makes the silence of the analyst the essential condition of her listening and of the patient eventually being able to speak from a place of regression.

The focus that Clerc gives the act of analytic listening is profound. It begins with the analyst's refusal to speak. Thus the analyst's refusal creates what in contemporary parlance would be called a 'virtual condition' from which the patient can depart the known, the expected and the real. For the analyst, her refusal also creates a space, one that allows her a place of imaginative activity separate from the patient's.[1] With these conditions in place, the analyst carefully listens to speech, apprehends images, imagines and engages with the charges associated with the words:

> The place of listening is that of the receiving surface of the psychic apparatus of the analyst, the Perception-Consciousness system becoming the surface excited by listening itself: what it perceives; but also what unfolds there, what the surface itself makes visible, what it allows to be imagined or guessed at, what it allows to be built. This time of apprehension of the speech of the other – in its forms, but also in the forms of its address – this time of perspective, is that of a palpation of surfaces . . . [where the] 'excited attention' (Kahn, 2001) of the analyst . . . [exists in] a psychic place constructed by listening . . . In the cure, it is the words which are the 'bearers' of the excitation effect, insofar as they are basically substitutes for the act, but it is the putting into words that 'slows down' the magic, it is [the analyst] who [as Lacoste (1999) has put it] 'restores to consciousness a time of seizure, a fragment of time torn from the omnipotence of thoughts'.
>
> (Clerc, 2007, p. 8)

This is something of a magical paragraph in itself. It speaks to the poet C. D. Wright's acknowledgement of her wish for identifiable content as well as her plea for poetry to take the 'formal acts' of language into account (2016, p. 88). Perhaps it even renders the divide between analysts who seek to find preformed unconscious content and those who see themselves as co-constructing content less meaningful. I am reminded of Winnicott's question about the transitional object: 'Did you find that or did you make that?' (1967). For in a way, the analytic set-up described by Clerc is reminiscent of the maternal dyad in which Winnicott wrote of the emergence of symbolic experience as it relates to separateness:

> I have claimed that when we witness an infant's employment of a transitional object, the first not-me possession, we are witnessing both the child's first use

of a symbol and the first experience of play. An essential part of my formulation of transitional phenomena is that we agree never to make the challenge to the baby: did you create this object, or did you find it conveniently lying around? That is to say, an essential feature of transitional phenomena and objects is a quality in our attitude when we observe them.

The object is a symbol of the union of the baby and the mother (or part of the mother). This symbol can be located. It is at the place in space and time where and when the mother is in transition from being (in the baby's mind) merged in with the infant and alternatively being experienced as an object to be perceived rather than conceived of. The use of an object symbolizes the union of two now separate things, baby and mother, *at the point in time and space of the initiation of their state of separateness.*

(1967, p. 369, my italics)

Our work takes place at this tipping point, where words, like transitional objects, encompass the movement from a place of being merged into a place of separateness. As Clerc suggests, it is a space not only of perception and reception but also of unfolding. As we traverse the frontier between these states, both in union with the patient and separate from her, we bring things with us in each border crossing.

Note

1 It is interesting to note the centrality of the notion of a separate space for Clerc and compare that with other intersubjective conceptualizations that emphasize relative experiences of merger, at-one-ment, overlapping or the existence of a field.

References

Bollas, C. (1993). *Being a Character: Psychoanalysis and Self Experience*. New York: Routledge.
Bollas, C. (2011). Character and Interformality. In: *The Christopher Bollas Reader*, A. Jemstedt (Ed.) pp. 238–248. New York: Routledge. .
Civitarese, G. (2013). 'The Inaccessible Unconscious and Reverie as a Path to Figurability.' In: H. Levine, G. Reed & D. Scarfone (Eds.) *Unrepresented States and the Construction of Meaning: Clinical and Theoretical Contributions*. London: Karnac Books, pp. 220–239.
Clerc, D. (2007). 'L'écoute de la parole.' *Revue Francaise de Psychanalyse*, 71(5): 1–114.
Freud, S. (1917). 'Introductory Lectures on Psychoanalysis. *S.E.*, Vol. 15, London: Hogarth Press, pp. 3–463.
Freud, S. (1926). 'The Question of Lay Analysis.' In: *Complete Works of Sigmund Freud*, Vol. XX, London: Hogarth Press, pp. 179–258.
Gentile, J. (2016). 'What Is Special About Speech?' *Psychoanalytic Psychology*, 33(1): 73–88.
Green, A. (1999). 'On Discriminating and Not Discriminating Between Affect and Representation.' *International Journal of Psychoanalysis*, 80: 277–316.
Greenberg, J. (1996). 'Psychoanalytic Words and Psychoanalytic Acts – A Brief History.' *Contemporary Psychoanalysis*, 32: 195–213.

Grossmark, R. (2018). 'Action Is Eloquence.' In: *The Unobtrusive Relational Analyst*. New York: Routledge.
Kahn, L. (2001). 'L'action de la forme.' *Bulletin de la SPP* (59): 983–1074.
Lacoste, P. (1999). *Barbarismes, L'inactuel. Formes du primitif.* Nouvelle série n° 3. Belfort: Circé.
Lafarge, L. (2014). 'How and Why Unconscious Phantasy and Transference Are the Defining Features of Psychoanalytic Practice.' *International Journal of Psychoanalysis*, 95(6): 1265–1278.
Langer, S.K. (1957). *Philosophy in a New Key*. (3rd ed.). Cambridge, MA: Harvard University Press.
Levine, H. (2013). 'The Colourless Canvas: Representation, Therapeutic Action, and the Creation of Mind.' In: H. Levine, G. Reed & D. Scarfone (Eds.) *Unrepresented States and the Construction of Meaning: Clinical and Theoretical Contributions*. London: Karnac Books, pp. 42–71.
Mead, G.H. (1934). *Mind, Self and Society*. C.W. Morris (Ed.). Chapter 11: Thought, Communication, and the Significant Symbol, pp. 68–74. Chicago: University of Chicago Press.
Miller, P. (2015). 'Piera Aulagnier, an Introduction: Some Elements of Her Intellectual Biography.' *International Journal of Psychoanalysis*, 96: 1355–1369.
Nettleton, S. (2017). *The Metapsychology of Christopher Bollas: An Introduction*. New York: Routledge.
Winnicott, D.W. (1967). 'The Location of Cultural Experience.' *International Journal of Psychoanalysis*, 48: 368–372.
Wright, C.D. (2016). *The Poet, the Lion, Talking Pictures, El Farolito, a Wedding in St. Roch, the Big Box Store, the Warp in the Mirror, Spring, Midnights, Fire & All*. Port Townsend, Washington: Copper Canyon Press.

Chapter 8

Duende and the shape of things unknown

> The *duende* ... Where is the *duende*? Through the empty archway a wind of the spirit enters, blowing insistently over the heads of the dead, in search of new landscapes and unknown accents: a wind with the odour of a child's saliva, crushed grass, and medusa's veil, announcing the endless baptism of freshly created things.
>
> 'Theory and Play of the *Duende*' – Federico Garcia Lorca (2001, p. 72)

How like poetry is psychoanalysis, our grasping for the unknown, our attempts to give words to experiences one can only hint at or make reference to by allusion. There are many realms in our lives: We may feel we exist differently at work, at home; in our relationships with friends, family and lovers; and there are also conscious and unconscious realms of experience. We move between these realms all the time, sometimes existing in them simultaneously. Our unconscious is perhaps the most mysterious realm of all, the one we keep attempting to domesticate by trying to relocate it in consciousness, which we do through understanding, narration or explanation. We say sometimes we are trying to connect to things beyond ourselves, when in reality, we are trying to connect with ourselves; we cannot do otherwise. I write 'beyond ourselves' in this way to indicate that the unconscious performs a double function in opening us to forces in the world that we can only feel but cannot know and aspects within us that seem go beyond who we think we are as selves.

In a brief essay, the poet Tracy K. Smith (2005) writes of the experience of living many lives simultaneously and draws on the poet Federico Garcia Lorca's idea of the 'Duende' to describe what for many of us will sound a familiar note. For Lorca, the figures of the muse and the angel exist outside of the poet, but the Duende exists inside and cannot be willed or controlled into service. In her essay, 'Survival in Two Worlds at Once' Smith writes,

> I love this concept of duende because it supposes that our poems are not things we create in order that a reader might be pleased or impressed (or, if

you will, delighted or instructed); we write poems in order to engage in the perilous yet necessary struggle to inhabit ourselves – our real selves, the ones we barely recognize – more completely. It is then that the Duende beckons, promising to impart 'something newly created, like a miracle', then it winks inscrutably and begins its game of feint and dodge, lunge and parry, goad and shirk; turning its back, nearly disappearing altogether, then materializing again with a bear-hug that drops you to the ground and knocks your wind out. You'll get your miracle, but only if you can decipher the music of the battle, only if you're willing to take risk after risk. Only, in other words, if you survive the effort. For a poet, this kind of survival is tantamount to walking, word by word, onto a ledge of your own making. You must use the tools you brought with you, but in decidedly different and dangerous ways.

The poet's work and the psychoanalyst's are not so different. Both court this miracle of creation, the glimpse of meaning in an experience that for a moment exists outside of consciousness. It is precarious work that, as Winnicott (1971a) observed, often poses a challenge to our psychic survival and requires particular analytic tools. Like the poet, we engage in this process not to delight or instruct, nor to please or impress, but rather, as Bion (1962) said, to get to the emotional truth of a session, a truth like the ones Smith describes, which are elusive and feel when they arrive as if they are miraculous.

Analyst and poet both open themselves to surviving in two worlds at once and to seeing what form those experiences will take. For patient and analyst both require a receptivity to the unknown and the unreasonable, to what no one wants to see or think or feel. For psychoanalysts, it may not be incidental that Lorca called the keeper of this dark realm the Duende, a name associated in Spanish and South American folklore with a demon, who as Garcia Lorca put it was the guardian of 'the mystery, the roots fastened in the mire that we all know and all ignore' (2001, p. 57). It is this guardian who allows the analyst his reveries, his 'crazy' dreams, and the madness that often takes monstrous forms in his mind. And it is from this place that interpretations gain their power if it is from there that they arise.

A great deal of emphasis is currently placed in psychoanalysis on the representation of unrepresented states. This focus, indicative of the analyst's increased attention to working with primitive mental states, massive psychic trauma and preverbal phenomena, is reflective of what Levine et al. (2013, p. 4) observe to be a sea change in the aims of psychoanalysis, which

> has begun to shift from conceiving solely or predominantly of a universe of presences, forgotten, hidden, or disguised but there for the finding, to a negative universe of voids where creation of missing structure, often referred to by the Freudian metapsychological designation, representation, becomes of necessity part of the cure.
> (e.g. Bion, 1970; Botella & Botella, 2005; Green, 1993, 1997; Roussillon, 1999; Winnicott, 1971)

Later in the same volume, Levine (2013, p. 44) further elaborates that

> what we are after may not yet have achieved a level of specificity and organization so as to be discernible and hidden; may not yet be embedded in a network of associated meanings; many not yet have achieved a specific form, and so may 'exist' only as a spectrum of possibilities that have yet to come into existence.

How like the elusive demon the Duende is the experience of the psychoanalytic process and of what we find, described by Smith, as one of feint and dodge, lunge and parry, goad and shirk, turning its back, nearly disappearing altogether and then materializing again with a bear hug that drops you to the ground and knocks your wind out. In the earlier quotation from Levine, we can see that, as in the poetic process, we wrestle with something that is not 'there', not hidden and not yet discernable, but something that will emerge. The Duende, in the words of Garcia Lorca, promises 'something newly created, like a miracle', though the psychoanalyst like the poet alike would regard this product as a moment in the 'endless baptism of freshly created things'.

At this point, we may ask what such a process is *for* and *why* psychoanalysts seek to give form to mental phenomena of this sort. The answer is quite complex and has to do with the ever-widening scope of psychoanalytic treatment as applied to severely character-disordered and psychotic individuals, and changing models of the mind that have resulted from clinical experiences of those treatments. I wish to focus on certain assumptions within these models, as they have created varied answers to the question of why the analyst believes they are engaged in the process of figurability. I begin with Bion and how his use of the word 'thinking' to describe the process by which the mother/analyst makes use of their own minds to contain and transform raw sensory experience (beta elements) through the application of alpha function leads to a model of treatment in which the aim becomes the development of structure that will allow the patient to 'think' his or her own experiences – i.e. be able to attribute meaning to phenomena existing at the level of unconsciousness. Bion (1967, p. 92) realized that clinically, it was crucial for a patient to 'put bad feelings in me and leave them there long enough for them to be modified by their sojourn in my psyche'. This move, as Brown (2011) explains, extended Klein's (1946) view of projective identification by emphasizing the communicative role of what the patient has evacuated in need of the analyst's modification and eventual return. This back and forth process of projection, containment, modification and return instantiates in the infant/patient what Bion (1962, p. 91) called an 'apparatus for thinking'. Yet there may be applied an unfortunate cognitivist quality to this focus on thinking, one that persists in influencing current day concepts growing out of his original approach to the development of the capacity to think (Fonagy et al., 2002).

Bion meant something quite original in his use of the term 'thinking', which practising psychoanalysts understand as having to do with the development of mind and the creation of meaning. Yet one can also see how putting the issue in these terms may potentially guide the psychoanalytic process in a particular direction such that what becomes valued is the cognitive-linguistic product of the process *rather than the process itself* – the symbolic representation over the creative experience. Even if this was not Bion's intention, as he has been understood more recently (Ogden, 2015) to have valued the joint experience of patient and analyst being at one with an unsettling psychic reality over the analyst's interpretation of that reality; nevertheless, this is one illustration of how the assumptions of a model may influence the analyst's conception of its aims.

In a rejoinder to Green's seminal work on the issue of representation, Ruth Stein (2001) offered a critique of his assumptions. Stein takes issue with the amount of attention ideational representation has received in analysts' notions of the construction of meaning, finding our reliance on this concept 'too static [and] atomistic'. She critiques Green's sole reliance on symbolic language 'to carry all the meaning' and believes this focus on representation is a vestige of Lacanian discourse theory. In an earlier paper, Stein (1999) addresses Green's construction of unconscious affect as lacking any 'qualities', citing his assertion that 'its transition to the unconscious state . . . would subject it to operations in which what gives it its psychical value would be missing'. But Stein (2001, original emphasis) argues,

> *Why would 'the unconscious' make quality disappear?* What is the theoretical obligation that forces us to such a view? What kind of an 'unconscious' is that: traversed by dark, nameless vectors of bodily tensions and unfelt but remembered ideas, repressed and multiplying, but *with no unconscious and meaningful feelings*?

She proposed broadening our conception of representation to include affect ('affect-representations') and interactive notions of representation as a procedure for re-experiencing. Stein's contribution can also be read as a critique of contemporary literature that follows from the work of Green and focuses on the symbolization of what are thought to be unrepresented states. Rather than viewing unconscious affective states as unrepresented, Stein considers that they already have 'qualities'. She advocates for an enlarged approach to the issue of representation, one that does not split affect from its constituent role in cognition, so it will

> stand in opposition to approaches that are content – or symbol – (or ideational-representation) centered, and . . . involves the recognition that affective phenomena are far more often employed as means of cognition than is generally recognized, that we cannot truly 'know' intense affective experiences unless we can identify them within ourselves, and that in human relationships *affective* communication is often the only way of 'knowing' another human being.
>
> (Ibid.)

Even though it should not need to be stated explicitly, Stein's approach to the issue of representation is not meant to replace the transformation of unconscious elements into symbolic narrative. She wished to open the concept of representation to include affect, while cognizant that doing so would have repercussions for matters of technique. Perhaps Stein's project was best described when Ogden (2005, p. 64) said that 'thinking frames the questions to be answered in terms of feelings'.

It would be interesting to extend Stein's critique to other analytic theories having to do with the representation of unconscious life. Were we to revisit Bion's conceptions of raw, unmetabolized beta elements, which include affective experience, we might theorize that beta elements, at least the affective ones, have 'qualities' and might already be a certain sort of affect representation. This line of thought makes logical sense if one considers beta elements must be transformed by alpha function into thinkable thoughts. In order for those thoughts to be referential to their source beta elements, the beta elements must have some qualities that would allow the communication of relevant emotional content. How else would an analyst know that her interpretation has anything to do with what is unconsciously occurring in the patient? An approach of this sort seems consistent with the way in which Levine earlier described states that have 'not yet . . . achieved a level of specificity and organization . . . may not yet have achieved a specific form, and so may exist only as a spectrum of possibilities that have yet to come into existence'. On this reading, such states may be understood not as unrepresented per se, but as liminal, with qualities that will submit themselves to, influence and take form within the psychoanalytic process.

C. Botella (2014) illustrates an approach to representation that may have one foot in each conceptualization – Green's and Stein's. Botella's work can be read as being both faithful to a more orthodox conceptualization in its treatment of unconscious affect as devoid of qualities, while at the same time heavily emphasizing, as Stein does, the central role of reliving an experience with the analyst that entirely has to do with affective expression and experiencing, without regard to issues of symbolization or ideational content. The reader can see how Botella toggles back and forth between an orthodox position and a revised position in the space of a page. He begins his piece by describing Freud as being 'less interested in the study of memory than in the *process of remembering*' (original italics). Botella then contrasts approaches focusing on the recovery of memory (i.e. reconstruction) with those focusing on experiences in the relationship with the analyst – that is to say the creation of new narratives, or experiences within the transference-countertransference through which early experience is recovered (i.e. constructed). He then elides this bifurcation in his own approach to remembering.

Drawing from Freud, he writes, 'It is . . . a primordial function of psychic life to create representations permitting the hitherto unrepresented trauma to be integrated within the representational networks' (ibid.). With this emphasis, Botella shifts the analytic enterprise to concentrate on the attribution of meaning to ahistorical unrepresented traumas, creating links between pre-psychic experiences and conscious knowing. Utilizing extensive italics to emphasize his idea, Botella writes of

> *a quantity of energy that has remained like a foreign body, without form or shape, without representation or memory, and even less meaning, and which can only be discharged through action or the hallucinatory activity of dreams by making use of any context whatsoever. Its content is more or less a matter of indifference; the only thing that counts is the repetition of the affect irrespective of the content used to convey it.*
>
> (Ibid.)

The impression given by this italicized quotation is that Botella follows Freud in emphasizing the *process* of remembering over the thing remembered. This process serves a function with regard to the 'quantity of energy' as a memory without recollection.[1] And rather than restricting this idea to those individuals who are understood to lack psychic structure Botella claims that such experiences 'nevertheless form part of each one of us'.

While Botella claims the content of such experiences is 'more or less a matter of indifference' and that it is the repetition of affect that is the most important factor, the clinical material he presents to support his approach relies heavily on what Stein termed 'symbol centered' representations arising from the analyst's process of 'regredience'. Botella (2014) offers his patient, Serge, a variety of interpretations about his past and is met with denial, rejection and disbelief until there is a moment in the treatment marked more by a change in affective tone than an understanding or accepting of history:

> There was a long moment of silence, and intense silence, though devoid of anxiety. Having recovered his composure, he said with astonishing calm: 'I feel I want to deny all that; I prefer not to think that my mother was not interested in what I was, that she didn't take account of the fact that I was a baby . . . it's not possible . . . I feel like minimizing all that.' A silence followed. This has a curious effect on me. 'I would prefer to think that everything you say is artificial . . . that you are the one who has invented all that.' Finally, he pulled himself together: 'But I have the clear memory now of having used the word *detrousser* when I was telling you the dream. I don't know if what you say is true, but I feel for the first time a real, great sense of calm.

For Botella, the reality of the memory arrived at is unrelated to its efficacy in organizing the patient's psychic equilibrium. It is the process of remembering, and not the memory, which leads to change.

Very much like Bion, or Ogden's (2015) reading of Bion, Botella's emphasis is placed not on the conscious understanding of what's been understood (the content or veracity of the thought or the memory) but on the unconscious process believed to have been occurring between patient and analyst prior to such understanding, the being at one with[2] or the process of *regredience*. Botella and Botella (2001) have written that regredience

> is a psychic state that includes quality and movement in an evolving process; it offers a potential for transformation, a permanent psychic capacity for transforming in an endo-hallucinatory manner any quantity of excitation, verbal, motor or emotional. The dream is its most accomplished manifestation.

This is perhaps preferable to the word 'thinking'. Botella draws on Freud's dream book (1900, p. 542) to describe a mode of psychic functioning characteristic of dreaming. Deeply process oriented, the idea of regredience returns us to the realm of the Duende in its exploration of what lies outside of language, symbolic or abstract thought. Allowing himself to regress so as to be receptive to the patient's unconscious the analyst 'works as a double' to him, using his capacities of figuration to transform his unconscious contents.

Ines

I received an anxious phone call from an older man who was concerned about his daughter, Ines. They came to see me in my consulting room. The father was clearly worried and had brought her to inquire about beginning treatment. As is not infrequent in such cases, by the time Ines had reached my office, she had hit rock bottom. She was in the throes of a major depression, had become dependent on benzodiazepines and marijuana and was on the verge of being asked to withdraw from her college. Minutes after our consultation began, I experienced a feeling of confusion that would become an important part of my early work with Ines. Her father said they were referred by a psychiatrist who had 'raved' about me and told him I was the person to consult. Her father had phoned me and set up the appointment as soon as possible after receiving this recommendation, as he was soon to return to the state in which he lived and wanted to make sure his daughter was being appropriately cared for.

I found myself flattered and confused. I had no idea who the psychiatrist was who had recommended me so highly. While Ines's father had repeated his name several times, it didn't sound familiar. Immediately I found myself thinking of other patients I was treating and had treated from the city where Ines had grown up. I wondered if there was some connection there. After this initial meeting, I also realized that neither had commented on the fact that they were different races – something I suspected I may not have known had I not seen them together for the initial consultation.

Treatment began intensively, with four sessions per week. Ines showed up to her sessions but she had very little to say. Her speech struck me as superficial and largely devoid of meaningful content or narrative. While she was clearly depressed, no tears accompanied her sadness. When I asked her a question about what she had said, she often deflected me with a light-hearted 'I don't know, whatever', and would grin like someone who had been anesthetized. For years, Ines had been on a regular diet of Xanax and marijuana, which had dulled her faculties. She saw no reason to discontinue her use of these substances; indeed, she embraced their effects. I found myself wondering who Ines was under the fog of her sedation, but had very little indication from what she began discussing with me.

Over some months, Ines did begin talking about 'topics', though it remained confusing to hear her speak of events about which she gave no background. She often switched who she was referring to without changing pronouns – e.g. at one time 'she' would refer to one friend and at another time someone else who had not been a character in the story so far. Fashion was one of her interests, so she routinely spoke about what her favourite performers wore in the various videos (in retrospect, I don't feel this choice was coincidental).

I found myself trying to follow along in my mind, wondering who a story was about, what had happened and what this meant to my patient, as there was little reflection with regard to these fragments. There was something about skateboards, a boy with many tattoos, a trip she wished to take or an article of clothing she would like to own and felt would look good. The partial intelligibility of these stories, mixed with their focusing on the most quotidian of elements, left me feeling dull. Increasingly, Ines bored me, and I began to dread her sessions. I asked her questions, attempted to make comments about her material and occasionally ventured into the realm of interpretation. However, the fact that I can recall none of these is a testament to my experience of how flat and useless they felt at the time, and how our entire interaction felt bereft of meaning or understanding.

In hindsight, it seems likely that this phase of our work was similar to a clinical phenomenon Cooper (2018) has written about regarding the intersubjective aspects of inevitable failures of symbolization, which occur when working with a patient whose capacities in this area are underdeveloped. As an experience in the transference-countertransference matrix, Cooper suggests the 'shared space in which patient and analyst feel deeply the failures of symbolization' serves to 'enact the impoverishment accompanying the patient's experience of object absence' with the analyst. I wouldn't know how valuable and applicable this idea was until sometime later.

Time passed, and it felt to me that Ines was settling into her analysis. While I continued to struggle with issues of boredom, confusion and disorientation, her presence was becoming familiar in a way that seemed beyond articulation or verbal understanding. Over time, I let go of attempts to *make sense* in my own mind of what she was saying, and as I did so, a memory occurred to me. I recalled numerous times when as a small boy I would visit my family in Europe and listen to my mother speak with her brothers and sisters in a language I didn't understand. I remembered the confusion of catching a word, eventually being able to piece together what topics they were talking about, but still not being able to follow what they were saying about those topics. As I sat with this memory, I realized that during those times, I felt bored, separate and alone. The unconscious communication from Ines had occurred well before the arrival of this memory of my own, which was the analytic mind work (Diamond, 2011) needed in order to make the communication a meaningful experience. Brown (2019, p. 3) has recently written that 'the analyst and patient are equally affected by the ambient emotion of the session but that each partner transforms it through his own storehouse of personal experiences and internal objects'. Being with Ines had called up this memory for me, and its arrival gave me the distance to consider my feelings of confusion and boredom as important to my patient's experience and the emotional truth of the hour.

I experimented with offering interpretations about an analyst feeling quite foreign to her and wondered if she felt confused by what was going on. Saying this felt very different, as if I were no longer commenting on something happening on an interpersonal level but describing something I felt to be true in Ogden's sense (2005):

> The analyst in making an interpretation (which has some truth to it and is utilizable by the patient) gives verbal 'shape' to experience that had once been non-verbal and unconscious. In so doing, the analyst creates the potential for a new experience of what is true which is derived from the patient's inarticulate unconscious experience.

Unexpectedly, the next week, Ines presented me with a poem she had written, and as the weeks went on, with a series of poems. They all had to do with her relationship with her mother and the feeling of precipitous separation from her. The first one read,

> Stitched in the sunset I bowed my head last night but never slept
> With threaded souls in different moons
> My mother and I will always remember
> Sleepless nights plush white pillows, the bath she gave me in another
> Woman's spoiled milk.
> She was an artist by death and I was a frozen statue
> Of body and silk by birth
> Her brown eyes reminded me that mine were brown too
> Together we were oil
> A gulf written in ink
> With words that spat out metal and smoke
> Before I was ready she lit a match and we exploded
> We became undone.
> I became the sky,
> My mother died.

Ines began to tell stories of a childhood living between the residences of her divorced parents. Her father had gone on to marry a much younger woman from

China, who spoke little to no English. Ines spent a lot of time with her while her father worked incessantly, returning from meetings with clients most nights well after dinner. Until this point, I had understood that the patient's mother was 'a brilliant writer'. Now I began to hear fragmented memories of Ines waking as a child in the middle of the night to find her mother labouring over another manuscript which would never be published. Her mother's behaviour was erratic and at times bizarre, and it soon became evident that she suffered from a long-standing depressive psychosis. She communicated her paranoias to the patient at an early age and was an inconstant presence, often disappearing for days at a time when she said she was stepping out for a couple of hours.

Ines's mother's incoherence left her daughter confused. Words didn't mean what they should, or they hung together to form unreliable thoughts. Increasingly, I came to think what Ines had communicated to me was her experience of her identification with her mother's madness, the confusion and disorientation of having been merged with a psychotic maternal object and the vicissitudes of experiencing that object as psychically absent (Green, 1983). I thought about my own memory of feeling separate from my mother as she spoke words I did not understand and how it was reflective of an experience of my patient having to do with how her mother's words were felt by her as what Joyce McDougall (1978) called an 'anti-communication' – i.e. a symptomatic *act*, repeated by the patient as speech not meant to communicate ideas but aiming at making the analyst feel something.

The sense of distance I remember feeling was akin to a distance Ines felt from a mother she was deeply connected to but separated from. As represented in the poem, an infantile fusion was exploded prematurely by her mother's madness, which felt like a death to the patient. With no one available to make sense of her world, a bereft Ines internalized the lost object and entered a state of melancholic identification (Freud, 1917). I explained these thoughts to the patient simply as things I had been thinking during our discussion, and for the first time since she'd begun her treatment, tears fell from her eyes and a different sort of sadness was expressed.

Grotstein (2004b, p. 111) wrote,

> When we view the unconscious from the vantage point of consciousness, we hypothesize 'instinctual drives' and 'internal objects'. But, when we view the objects of consciousness from within the domain of the unconscious, we are face-to-face with 'phantoms', 'demons' (both positive and negative), 'spirits', 'angels', and a whole lexicon of numinous preternatural 'presences', all holographically intermixed with external objects.

For Garcia Lorca, the demon expressed as the Duende exerted its force on this treatment, dulling the participants awareness and inculcating memories without recollection (Botella, 2014). The period of Ines's analysis described here brought her infantile experience of object absence to the transference-countertransference

(Bollas, 1983) and consequently returned me to a childhood memory in order to learn more than I had been able to know of my own experience so that I could bring that to bear on a present experience of the patient's past. I would say, in agreement with Botella, that it was the process of remembering that was more important than what was remembered, even if it is difficult for me to entirely say that the content of these memories was more or less a matter of indifference. The shape that was given to Ines's affective experience, already an experience of a 'quality', felt to me to be the most powerful mutative element because there was a feeling of analytic truth to this shape. It was a truth that eventually would move Ines out of her melancholic identification into grieving and down from the sky.

Notes

1 Scarfone (2014) notes such an approach to memory to be consistent throughout Freud's work, from 'On Aphasia' (1891) through 'The Project' (1895) and including his letter to Fliess of 6 December 1896. He concludes that for Freud, 'memory was never simply made of memories (or recollections) and that "the work of remembering" is more and something else than being able to produce a narrative of things past'.
2 Bion's idea of 'being-at-one with' has been interpreted in various ways. Grotstein (2004a), for instance, has rejected the idea that it involves a fusion with the patient and loss of ego boundaries, even in a transitory manner. Eshel (2017), however, believes these to be important aspects of the analyst's experience of being-at-one with.

References

Bion, W.R. (1962). *Learning from Experience*. London: Heinemann.
Bion, W.R. (1967). 'On Arrogance.' In: *Second Thoughts*. New York: Jason Aronson, pp. 86–92.
Bion, W.R. (1970). *Attention and Interpretation*. London: Tavistock Publications.
Bollas, C. (1983). 'Expressive Uses of the Countertransference.' *Contemporary Psychoanalysis*, 19: 1–33.
Botella, C. (2014). 'On Remembering: The Notion of Memory Without Recollection.' *International Journal of Psychoanalysis*, 95: 911–936.
Botella, C. & Botella, S. (2001). 'Regredience et figurabilite. Report to the Congress for French-Speaking Analysts, Paris.' *Revue Française de Psychanalyse*, 4: 1148–1239.
Botella, C. & Botella, S. (2005). *The Work of Psychic Figurability: Mental States Without Representation (The New Library of Psychoanalysis)*. A. Weller & M. Zerbib (Trans.). London: Routledge.
Brown, L. (2011). *Intersubjective Processes and the Unconscious*. New York: Routledge.
Brown, L. (2019). *Transformational Processes in Clinical Psychoanalysis: Dreaming, Emotions and the Present Moment*. New York: Routledge.
Cooper, S.H. (2018). *Playing in the Darkness: Use of the Object and Use of the Subject*. Keynote Address, American Psychoanalytic Association. 16 February.
Diamond, M. (2011). 'The Impact of the Mind of the Analyst: From Unconscious Process to Intrapsychic Change.' In M. Diamond & C. Christian (Eds.). *The Second Century*

of Psychoanalysis: Evolving Perspectives on Therapeutic Action. London: Karnac, pp. 205–235.

Eshel, O. (2017). 'From Extension to Revolutionary Change in Clinical Psychoanalysis: The Radical Influence of Bion and Winnicott.' *Psychoanalytic Quarterly*, 86(4): 753–794.

Fonagy, P., Gergely, G., Jurist, E.L. & Target, M. (2002). *Affect Regulation, Mentalization, and the Development of the Self*. New York: Other Press.

Freud, S. (1891). *On Aphasia: A Critical Study*. Stengel, E. (Trans.). New York, NY: International UP, 1953.

Freud, S. (1895). 'Project for a Scientific Psychology.' *S.E.*, Vol. 1, London: Hogarth Press, pp. 281–397.

Freud, S. (1917). 'Mourning and Melancholia.' *S.E.*, Vol. 14, London: Hogarth Press, pp. 239–248.

Garcia Lorca, F. (2001). 'Play and Theory of the Duende.' In: *In Search of Duende*. New York: New Directions Books.

Green, A. (1983). 'The Dead Mother.' In: *Private Madness*. Madison, CT: International Universities Press, 1980, pp. 142–173.

Green, A. (1993). *The Work of the Negative*. A. Weller (Trans.). New York: Free Association Books, 1999.

Green, A. (1997). 'The Intuition of the Negative in Playing and Reality.' *International Journal of Psychoanalysis*, 78: 1071–1084.

Grotstein, J.S. (2004a). 'The Seventh Servant: The Implications of a Truth Drive in Bion's Theory of "O".' *International Journal of Psychoanalysis*, 85(5): 1081–1101.

Grotstein, J.S. (2004b). 'The Light Militia of the Lower Sky: The Deeper Nature of Dreaming and Phantasying.' *Psychoanalytic Dialogues*, 14: 99–118.

Klein, M. (1946). 'Notes on Some Schizoid Mechanisms.' In: *Envy and Gratitude*. London: Hogarth Press, 1975, pp. 1–24.

Levine, H., Reed, G. & Scarfone, D. (2013). *Unrepresented States and the Construction of Meaning: Clinical and Theoretical Contributions*. London: Karnac.

Levine, H. (2013). 'The Colourless Canvas: Representation, Therapeutic Actin, and the Creation of Mind.' In: H. Levine, G. Reed & D. Scarfone (Eds.) *Unrepresented States and the Construction of Meaning: Clinical and Theoretical Contributions*. London: Karnac, pp. 42–71.

McDougall, J. (1978). 'Primitive Communication and the Use of Countertransference – Reflections on Early Psychic Trauma and Its Transference Effects.' *Contemporary Psychoanalysis*, 14: 173–209.

Ogden, T.H. (2005). 'What's True and Whose Idea Was It?' In: *This Art of Psychoanalysis*. New York: Routledge, pp. 61–76.

Ogden, T.H. (2015). 'Intuiting the Truth of What's Happening: On Bion's 'Notes on Memory and Desire.' *Psychoanalytic Quarterly*, LXXXIV(2): 285–306.

Roussillon, R. (1999). *Agonie clivage et symbolization*. Paris: Presses Universitaires de France. [Primitive Agony and Symbolization. London: Karnac Books, 2011.]

Scarfone, D. (2014). 'The Work of Remembering and the Revival of the Psychoanalytic Method.' *International Journal of Psychoanalysis*, 95: 965–972.

Smith, T.K. (2005). Survival in Two Worlds at Once: Federico Garcia Lorca and Duende. Website: Poets.org.

Stein, R. (1999). *Le transfer n'est plus ce qu'il etait*. Rev. Franc Psychanal, Monographie de Psychanalyse: Transferts, pp. 101–116.

Stein, R. (2001). 'Affect in Psychoanalytic Theory.' *International Journal of Psychoanalysis*, 82(5): 877–900.

Winnicott, D.W. (1971a). *The Use of an Object and Relating Through Identification Playing and Reality*, ed. New York: Basic Books, pp. 86–94 (Original work published 1969).

Winnicott, D.W. (1971). 'Transitional Objects and Transitional Phenomena.' In: *Playing and Reality*. London: Tavistock Publications, pp. 1–25.

Chapter 9

Creative repetition

Introduction

This chapter is about the power of creative transformation that is to be found in Freud's (1920) observation of the Fort/Da, which is not simply about mastery by way of the ego's omnipotence but towards the growth of the individual. Rather than approach repetition as a difficulty to be transcended, I will argue that repetition is the vehicle of its own transcendence. For, if action is not to be separated from the psychic processes of the patient, which are themselves forms of action (Loewald, 1965) or from the psychoanalytic dyad, within which action is a constant variable (Reis, 2010), then this chapter explores the possibility of different outcomes for the resolution of repetition than symbolic thought.

I've chosen to approach the topic of repetition, an everyday topic that presents itself with every session in order to ground the hour in a repetition of the past and foreclose the possibility of new experiencing, so as to illustrate its relation with other motives Freud (1920, p. 37) referred to in 'Beyond the Pleasure Principle', 'which push forward towards progress and the production of new forms'. This chapter will describe an unfolding process of unconscious intersubjective negotiation where early conservative repetition yields to repetition that carries the potential for progress and the production of new forms. I illustrate that within the countertransference, the analyst's experience of pleasure may provide a conduit for the reception of a message sent by the patient addressed to the object and that the mode of reception is all important (Reis, 2009).

Varieties of repetition

Freud found pleasure in repetition – in children's wordplay, 'the pleasurable effect of rhythm and rhyme' (1905, p. 125), and in the ways children delight in re-experiencing something identical, such as hearing the same story over and over again (1920, p. 36). He linked the act of remembering to pleasure (1905, p. 122) and remembering and repetition to the telling of jokes (1905, p. 231). These sources of pleasure – rhyming, storytelling, joke telling and even reflecting – all represented for Freud benign forms of repetition.

But repetition has its dark side as well. And when it becomes compulsive, Freud saw in it something 'daemonic' (1920, p. 36) that was not seen to bring pleasure; this form of repetition appeared to stand outside or beyond the pleasure principle and was guided by a conservative force seeking to drive us backwards rather than forward, to limit us rather than expand us. In 'Beyond the Pleasure Principle' (1920), Freud introduced us to three varieties of compulsive repetition. The first variety is what today we would consider posttraumatic stress disorder, and what he called 'traumatic neurosis' or war neurosis'. In this condition, the patient is delivered 'back into the situation of his accident', and 'the strength of that experience' is repeatedly forced upon him in his dream and waking life. It is as if the individual reencounters the surprise of his trauma and is unprepared each time it repeats. He is 'fixated to his trauma' (p. 13), writes Freud, and whether it is an accident or a battlefield he finds the individual psychologically arrested at the time of its occurrence.

Freud then introduced hysteria as a second variety of repetition compulsion which he feels follows a trauma and is also marked by fixation. 'Fixations to the experience which started the illness' (1920, p. 13) he stated, are, of course, familiar to him by this time. He cited his own work with Breuer (1893) on hysteria, recalling the famous phrase that 'hysterics suffer mainly from reminiscences'. Leaving aside the intriguing statement that seems to contradict his famous letter of May 1897 to Fliess, where he renounced his seduction theory, Freud compared the symptoms of the hysteric to those of the patient with war neurosis and observed that his colleagues Ferenczi and Simmel 'have been able to explain certain motor systems by fixation to the moment at which the trauma occurred' (p. 13).

Confronted with traumatized soldiers returning from WWI, accident and sexual assault victims, Freud worked to accommodate their posttraumatic symptoms to the model of neuroses he had developed. As their dreams did not take the form of wish gratifications, and their behaviour was not that of neurotic conflict between the pleasure and reality principles, he struggled to modify his previous conceptualizations. 'In the past', writes Lear (2005, p. 159),

> Freud told us that these acts had hidden gratifications; that they were disguised wish-fulfilments and compromise formations. Now he tells us that they lead only to unpleasure . . . In effect, Freud is saying that much of an analysand's behavior in the transference must be understood in a new way. But if his theory of transference needs to be revised, so does his account of therapy and cure.

Freud posited another force at work, a 'conservative instinct' (1920, p. 37) underlying these first two forms of traumatic repetition, that of a primordial compulsion to repeat. Posttraumatic conditions, Freud suggested, thus return the solider, the victim of the accident and the hysteric to the battlefield, the scene of their accident or the scene of their seduction. Moreover, because of the failure of the ego to bind the free flow of energy, to channel and contain it, what compulsively repeats does so unchanged, escaping understanding and remaining unprocessed or unfiltered by the experience of the self (Scarfone, 2011, p. 84). Little wonder that on this understanding, analysts beginning with Freud (1920, p. 16) have tended to focus their efforts at resolution around the ego's mastery, its ability to order and give meaning to experience and the reasons for its loss of control.

If the first two forms of compulsive repetition Freud introduces are posttraumatic reactions, I would suggest the third form to be the introduction of neurotic repetition. In transitioning from the theme of traumatic repetition to what he considered the developmentally normal experiences in the play of children, Freud writes,

> At this point I propose to leave the dark and dismal subject of the traumatic neurosis and pass on to examine the method of working employed by the mental apparatus in one of its earliest normal activities – I mean in children's play.
>
> (1920, p. 14)

Consequently, the third variety of repetition comes through the example of his grandson's invention of the Fort/Da game, in which the child repeats the unpleasure of his mother's departure, 'compensat[ing] for this, as it were, by himself staging the disappearance and return of the objects within his reach' (1920, p. 15).

There are several factors that would seem to distinguish this form of repetition from the previous two. In addition to repetition as return, Freud also considered the creative invention of the game as the child's 'reply' to his mother leaving and a sort of preparation for her joyful return, a feature I will take up in more detail shortly. Freud's focus seems to largely centre on the child's active development of mastery of the experience. He writes that the child 'enacts' the mother's departure in a repetitive manner and that this is the 'true purpose of the game' (pp. 15–16), a purpose he links to the development of the symbolic capacity in the child to represent his mother's absence. In this variety of repetition, he added that there is another way the individual may achieve mastery over the experience: not only can the child attempt to take active mastery over his experience by enacting it under the sway of a wish (as illustrated in the Fort/Da game) but also he can transfer the experience: 'He hands on the disagreeable experience to one of his playmates and in this way revenges himself on a substitute' (p. 17).

If the first two posttraumatic varieties of repetition produced only unpleasure, I read Freud as distinguishing the third variety of compulsive repetition by its generating pleasurable effects.

He writes that in this form of repetition compulsion, even though it is the repetition of an unpleasant situation, there must also be 'a yield of pleasure' (p. 16). Thus in addition to his focus on attempts at the mastery of such situations, the child's repetition is also seen by Freud to be influenced by a wish. The wish may be a hostile one that the child actively takes charge of in throwing the spool away and/or it may be a wish for mother's joyful return. In both cases, however, there is a yield of pleasure. One reason this is remarkable is that Freud has already told us the victim of the accident or war derives no gratification of wishes from their dreaming; dreaming itself is 'diverted from its purposes' (p. 13) and can no longer help the individual resolve their situation, only repeat it.

That Freud posited the pleasurable effect of compulsive repetition in this third form complicates a simple dichotomous approach to the issue of pleasure/unpleasure. Indeed, I would contend that his linking both to compulsive repetition brings these terms into closer relation than either of them stand in relation to the issue of satisfaction. As Freud progressed in his investigation of children's play, this area too began to take on complication as he acknowledged that there are many determinants that go into constituting it, 'other motives' in addition to the compulsion to repeat and that it is difficult to know which are primary, or even which are present.

This chapter will take up the experience of the third sort of repetition in clinical psychoanalysis with an eye towards these other motives, for in addition to 'the conservative instincts which impel towards repetition', Freud also posited the existence of 'others which push forward towards progress and the production of new forms' (1920, p. 37). I will seek to illustrate what is necessary for the shift from the patient's using the analyst as an object of repetition to an object of play. I distinguish my approach from more traditional approaches to the subjects of enactment (Steiner, 2006) or actualization (e.g. Sandler, 1976; Green, 2000) by suggesting new perspectives from which to view these phenomena.

The topic of pleasure will be examined as an aim of what Winnicott (1971) called primary creativity and contrasted with the pleasure of wish fulfilment. For if, as the poet suggested, 'The heart asks pleasure first, and then, excuse from pain' (Dickinson, 2000), then here I suggest a developmental course for the normal experience and expression of pleasure, one that if not impinged upon may unfold over the progression of normal development to satisfaction, but one that also has the possibility of being taken over by the ego's wish to master unpleasure through a repetition that carries a yield of pleasure.

Pleasure and the playground

Michael Parsons (2014) notes that the roots of Winnicott's ideas having to do with playing as an intermediate, transitional area can be found in Freud's solution to repetition compulsion. He observed in 'Remembering, Repeating and Working Through' (1914) that Freud used the same words as Winnicott (1971a, p. 50) in describing what is necessary to establish an individual's creative living. Freud noted that repetition becomes 'harmless and indeed useful [when we] giv[e] it the right to assert itself in a definite field' (1914, p. 154). For Freud, this field is the transference, where repetition compulsion is

> admit[ted] . . . into the transference as a playground in which it is allowed to expand in almost complete freedom . . . the transference thus creates an

intermediate region between illness and real life, through which the transition from one to the other is made.

(Ibid.)

One clearly and immediately sees the parallel Parsons has discovered: how Freud's intermediate regions of the transference as a vehicle for the transition from illness to reality resemble Winnicott's intermediate, transitional area of experiencing, a playground which may open to an experience of creative living or freedom from compulsion.[1]

The first two examples of traumatic repetition quite naturally lead clinicians to focus their therapeutic efforts on fostering the symbolization of early inchoate or traumatically blocked experiences. Elsewhere, I've written on an analytic approach to working with these forms of post-traumatic repetition (Reis, 2009). In this approach, memory is central, and its expression becomes a focus. Clinicians from all psychoanalytic schools have sought to make thinkable such experiences, to transition them from unconscious thought to language, and hence to conscious understanding. However, the third form of repetition is of a neurotic type, different from the first two in significant ways and best treated when it enters the playground of the transference-countertransference, resuming an early form of enactive play. In this sort of repetition, there seems to be a component of the first two types Freud identified, a concrete repetitiveness. But the third variety of repetition identified by Freud seems to contain something additional. Added to the repetitiveness is a creative act that appears to aim not simply at mastery by way of the ego's omnipotence but towards the growth of the individual. The inclusion of play opens a possibility that links repetition to a creative act of invention (Caruth, 2013) – one that seeks to free pleasure from its having been yoked to compulsive repetition. Thus the focus of therapeutic efforts in the third form will not first be on symbolizing what is repeated or relived, or on further empowering the ego through activity or omnipotence, but on creating the conditions for having a new experience.

Clinical illustration

Sylvie is a nose; that is the professional designation for someone who has been trained to identify and combine the olfactory elements needed to create the world's most luxurious perfumes. In her early adulthood, she attended an unusual school outside of Paris from which most graduates join the ranks of the great perfume houses, going on to develop the scents that will be marketed and distributed by global brands. There she learned to combine fragrances and make minute changes to the molecular formulations of perfumes. While her classmates followed a path into a corporate life, Sylvie decided to take a different path and became a consultant. She worked with boutique hotels to create signature scents for their properties, with celebrities and the ultra-rich, who desired perfumes created to their own specifications and liking. While she attained considerable success over the years, she complained that she 'felt nothing' and that her accomplishments were empty of any feeling of satisfaction, despite 'having made it to the top of my field'.

Her professional life meant that she moved in circles with billionaires and movie stars, and as her analysis began, she told stories saturated with the atmosphere of bacchanalia and excess in which she conducted her business. Decades earlier, she had been considered a great beauty, tall and elegant, which allowed her to move effortlessly in a world of celebrity and wealth. Looking back on her early life left her with a feeling of sad nostalgia for having been unable to appreciate all she was involved in. There was something intriguing about hearing Sylvie's descriptions of the scents that a rock-and-roll icon favored and how she spent time walking around with him, determining which smells appealed as they ambled through the city of London or the woods around his house. I also felt that same intrigue upon hearing of trips to China where her unique scent creations became a marker of status for very rich women who could afford her bespoke services and how an elite hotel in Barcelona engaged her to create an olfactory atmosphere that would convey what they felt to be their unique brand of luxury. These seemed to me special and rare experiences, and in their telling, they had a pleasingly seductive flavor. She explained what had made her highly successful was crafting different scents for different regions. The Chinese liked light and airy, the Russians rich and heavy, the Brazilians fruity and floral. Her status as a one-woman operation allowed her to craft particular scents to these varying preferences years before the big perfume houses followed suit. While listening, I became aware that an experience had been created within me, and alongside what I felt to be a growing admiration for this patient's unique talents and skills, I knew another process had unconsciously begun to take shape.

As I prefer to work within the transference and feel no urgency to rush to understandings, I consistently chose not to interpret or explicitly raise questions about her use of these experiences vis-à-vis the analyst. Although my interest was often piqued, I said little during these associative reminiscences, noting when I could the tantalizing appeal of these tales of glamour, yet not remarking on them or asking the many questions that came to my mind about rock stars and royalty.

Over time, I learned that my choice to say little was guided by an unconscious intuition. As the alluring tales began to yield, stories of misery and alienation in childhood became more prominent. She had grown up in an unhappy home. Her parent's marriage suffered from chronic opposition, and the strain left her mother depressively collapsed for most of her daughter's childhood. The patient's mother's mood alternated between hostile glowering at her husband and a pervasive gloomy dullness. The only things that seemed to rouse her from her leaden state were the 'shows' Sylvie would put on for her. The patient recalled that her mother would brighten briefly during her daughter's performances, and sometimes, Sylvie remembered, she smiled or even laughed before reentering a somber and grim space. Because of his work and affairs with other women, Sylvie remembered her father as an infrequent presence. Yet the regular charm of his personality quickly turned to callousness with his wife. Sylvie felt warm towards her father, who she felt treated her especially exuberantly, until adolescence when she began to feel uncomfortable that his attention towards her had become sexualized. Remarkably, each of her memories as they unfolded was dappled with accompanying scents – of the heavy woollen blanket she would hold close during her parents arguments, of her father's musky smell when returning home in the heat of the late afternoon from who knows where, of what it smelled like to sit silently with her mother while rain fell outside. Sylvie had partially retreated from the world of object relating and found a refuge in the sensorium (Aulagnier, 1986).

In the terms Freud applied to the third form of repetition, Sylvie repeated in the transference her attempts at mastering an early situation of unhappiness, attempting to enliven the analyst as the depressed object for whom she would put on a show. Under the sway of the wish, these tales of glamour and intrigue were ultimately voyeuristic and empty, and I had the feeling that she was telling me these things as she might to a room full of people – that is to say, not particularly to me, her analyst, but in an impersonal, social manner. The stories Sylvie told were a repetition, a putting on of a show, but not playing in a Winncottian sense. Because this play was still yoked to compulsive repetition (i.e. tantalization), its aim was ego mastery of an internal experience through wish fulfilment, and its creative aspect remained arrested. By saying little about them, I was also showing her that they would not overwhelm me to the point of creating a major transference-countertransference enactment, wherein the story can become a way of turning life into a deadened object or playing at Oedipal seduction. At the same time, I conjectured that Sylvie already knew at an unconscious level, and perhaps from her previous experiences with others, that such stories were affecting and that she had tantalized me. Similar to what Carpy (1989) has described, Sylvie was witnessing my capacity to tolerate her affective impact without my grossly acting out in response or offering interpretations. For Carpy, such subtle enactments, in which a patient can tell the analyst is affected and observe the mental work they are doing to metabolize these effects, is viewed as similar to the inevitability of a mother showing her infant that she is affecting the mother while at the same time allowing her to observe the mother's attempts to deal with these feelings. I understand the position of the analyst when working in this manner to be consistent with Winnicott's emphasis on non-impingement and survival of the patient's experience and thus chose to not interpret and potentially arrest, but rather contain an unfolding process.

Sylvie went on to speak about the sadness of her early life and the lack of satisfaction she felt internally. Over time, we discussed a disappointing history of relationships and her sense that of the things missing in her childhood, kindness felt particularly lacking. Her romantic partners had been exciting, powerful people, but not people she would call kind. Together, we understood that Sylvie had gotten lost in her own show by continuing to perform her life in a stylized manner focused on the needs of others. She considered that her own adult relationships may have masochistically recreated her parents' unhappy coupling in the familiar pattern of each partner punishing the other for not meeting their needs. Her masturbatory fantasies revolved around sexual masochism, which highlighted the unkindness of others. She spent her life carefully, creatively crafting aesthetic experiences for others and felt personally unsatisfied and unappreciated in the process.

During the third year of analysis, on a day that did not seem particularly remarkable, Sylvie, who had been consulting with a group of investors who wanted to open a bar in downtown Manhattan, was associatively going through a list of concerns, speaking about details of her contract with the group and complications in hiring and training bartenders. By this time, she had begun to be able to associate, and it was not uncommon that she would freely speak about the various matters on her mind and be able to follow them to identify unconscious themes. She was hired to develop the cocktail list, and in characteristic fashion, she began to detail the lengths she'd gone to in developing the drinks. These were cocktails thought out to a remarkable degree – not just with respect to their rare and fine ingredients, and the way these ingredients were combined but also with respect to the history of popular cocktails and recent styles of preparation. As she conceived them, they were extraordinarily creative, and as she described them from the couch, I felt something unusual happening to me: a feeling of profound pleasure quite literally filled me from head to toe; it was nothing less than a visceral sensation of acute joy.

It may help to know that cocktails are on the short list of things that delight me. So when she described in some considerable detail formulations using extract of saffron, mint and rose, powdered orris root and the flavors of green mango, lavender and black pepper, in order to find just the right note, my attitude shifted from one of interest to intense enjoyment. While I feel quite sure that Sylvie had no indication of this reaction in me, there felt to me something delightful about what she was describing and about what was going on inside me – I would even say about what was going on between us.

Sylvie continued talking about walking in the neighbourhood where the bar was going to open. She wanted to smell the crumpled leaves, the aromas emerging from restaurants, dry cleaners and people's windows that would contribute to the architecture of the various drinks she was formulating. Since the neighbourhood bordered New York's Chinatown, she visited the outdoor markets there, smelling the dragon fruit, papaya, lychee and tamarind. Then, in discussing the cocktails themselves, she described how she had tasted numerous varieties of gin before deciding to use a Spanish producer for a variation on a martini she had created. In making her decision, she had combined each gin with various ingredients, going through a palate of flavors before settling on one choice. The process was precise, deliberate and intensive. Fascinated, I uttered words I never had before and am likely never to utter again in an analytic session: '*Spanish* gin?!' I said quizzically. She laughed and picked up immediately on the affect permeating the question. 'Yes!' she replied. The gin made in Spain was different from most others, on the nose, it held hints of violet, sweet orange, coriander and had a floral brightness. Sylvie continued to describe this gin with a sort of rapt bliss. While she felt it leaned slightly towards citrus, she also felt it had another side to it, deeper notes of nutmeg, cinnamon and cardamom. She described that the taste begins quietly until the aromatics re-enter the nose. Then the middle begins with fresh bright juniper, turning crisper and bolder. But the finish was what set the Spanish gin apart: it was really bright, a touch sweet and strongly aromatic, with cardamom, angelica, nutmeg and a wide array of baking spices with sharper licorice and fennel on the finish. This was a new type of gin, she explained, far from the British or North American gins of the last decades. And to adorn the martini, she used sprigs of fresh rosemary that she had been growing in window boxes outside of her apartment over the past months. 'That's fascinating', I said and added that this was the first I'd heard of her growing her own herbs. She told me it made a significant difference to the taste of the drink if the rosemary was picked just a few hours before it was used, and so she had decided to grow a batch herself, but she hadn't thought to mention it to me. I commented on how she seemed to put such careful thought into each ingredient and into how each ingredient compliments and plays off the others and the surroundings. She responded, 'For me, it's sort of like music, layering one melody on top of another'. She continued by adding that the boutique hotel in Barcelona had asked her to put together a playlist of music that would pair with the scents she had developed for them, and she carefully selected and sequenced the pieces: 'It's like writing, one sentence, then another and then you have a paragraph'. I said that it struck me with regard to the scents, the drinks and the music that she was conveying something to others that was mostly out of their awareness – that the subtlety of her creations was very likely registered by others at some level, but most likely in a way that was not conscious. With emotion reflective of a sense of joyful discovery, Sylvie remarked, 'It's a sort of communication, I guess!' 'Yes', I said, 'that seems exactly right'.

Discussion

Rather than approaching the clinical process described here as a series of enactments or as a failure of countertransference reflectiveness, it may be viewed differently through more contemporary lenses. For instance, from a relational perspective, Cooney (2018, p. 340) recently proposed the conception of 'vitalizing enactments', seeing the possibility in enactment for 'a progressive and creative lived experience, rather than an unconscious collision to be survived and symbolized'. Drawing largely on the work of Alvarez (2012) Cooney viewed vitalizing enactment to be a 'lived process [that] is itself transformative' (p. 351) and did not necessarily seek symbolization or understanding. Central to her conception is the idea that analyst and analysand are from the beginning of their work together always in unconscious dialogue and, following Alvarez, that the analytic container can be a medium for the transformation of nascent feelings of love, joy and hope as much as for conflict and painfully dissociated affect.

From a Bionian field theory perspective, Peltz (2018) took a more critical view of the conception of enactment itself, seeing it as limiting: 'I think we are still rather haunted by the privileged status of representation and the capacity for symbolization, viewing other more direct experiences as lesser and indicative of more disturbance' (p. 366). In her reading of the recent evaluation of the concept of enactment by Bohleber et al. (2013), Peltz remarked that the historical injunction for 'speech not action' had the potential to 'restrict the ways we hear (Peltz, 2012) and respond to what's happening in the analytic field when we are not in the symbolic register' (p. 364). Thus Peltz concluded,

> For lack of a more refined and specific metapsychological language to explore the *alternative channels* for registering the patient's communications, we have been left with – and reduced to – the concept of enactment, which remains limited and unnecessarily fraught due to the history and evolution of this term.
>
> (p. 366, original emphasis)

Mindful that the approach she sought to further explore was a slippery slope, Peltz carefully took a position that eschewed an absence of rigor or an unreflective 'wild' stance. Rather, she sought to further theorize what she called, following the contributions of Alvarez, the 'contacting' dimension of our work, the ways in which we reach towards our patients that are not necessarily about understanding, symbolization or interpreting but will inevitably involve the subjective unconscious involvement of the analyst as well as patient.

One aspect of Peltz's work I would like to highlight for the present investigation has to do with her wish to broaden the analytic conversation past what she viewed as a narrowing conception of enactment to include 'moving/high-risk encounters' (p. 364). As examples, she cited the use of unsaturated interpretations by field theorists and joining patients within registers of the nonverbal, the rhythmic, the gestural and the expressive – i.e. the languages they speak and the mediums through which they communicate (one may think here of Balint's (1968) work as well). There is also a strong similarity to the conceptualization of 'moments of meeting' from the Boston Change Process Study Group (2010) that often take place outside of the usual and expected mode of analytic interaction and represent an experiential sharing and fittedness wherein both participants sense that new and different possibilities for relating are opening up between them. These differing analytic approaches all appear to be describing heightened moments in the treatment. I would like to emphasize that these moments result from the analytic process that precedes them, and as such, they are products of that process. By taking a process-oriented approach, as I do in this chapter, one may be less likely to regard Sylvie's treatment as an isolated series of enactments and more likely to see an unfolding process of unconscious intersubjective negotiation, where early conservative repetition yields to repetition that carries the potential for progress and the production of new forms.

For Winnicott (1974), the experience of being tantalized was considered more destructive than a situation of deprivation and 'perhaps the worst thing that can happen to a baby'. While the tantalizing dynamic had taken up an early residence within the transference-countertransference I was conscious of the need to avoid allowing its full enactment and to differentiate myself by allowing the patient to see the mental work I was doing to moderate my own reactions (that is to say, how she was unconsciously attempting to use me as an object of repetition). When such moments occur, as they often do earlier in a treatment, they create vulnerabilities for enactment, as they are more traditionally understood, since they arise prior to the development of an unconscious intersubjective relation that will allow new forms to emerge as repetition expands 'in almost complete freedom within the unconscious dimensions of the transference-countertransference' (Freud, 1914, p. 154). It is the development of that process, however, that will allow repetition to take the form of a communication for an analyst who is newly created by the patient as an object of play.

The experience of discussing cocktails with this patient was instead a form of deep communication from what Bollas would call the patient's character, by which he means a pattern of being and relating generated by her unique idiom. Bollas (2011, p. 243) writes,

> To receive another's character requires an unconscious decision on the recipient's part to allow this. This decision may be communicated as the intelligence of reception, the capacity to allow the self to be impressed by the other. The roots of this capacity are pleasurable; they reside in the mother's receptive relation to her infant, and we carry it forward as adults in the way we enjoy receiving other people and the object world. To engage this receptiveness in the psychoanalytic space the analyst must empty his mind, to be in Bion's terms 'without memory or desire', so that unconscious character-perception is possible.
>
> (p. 243)

There has been little attention given to the analyst's experience of pleasure or joy, as the majority of focus has been on what the analyst has had to undergo that has been depriving and painful, and had to be endured (Shulman, 2016; Heisterkamp, 2001). More specifically, amongst those who have contributed greatly to our understanding of countertransference experiences of repetition (Rosenfeld, 1987; Schafer, 2003; Green, 2005, 2011), Cooper (2015) noted that there has been little focus on the analyst's experience of pleasure. Alvarez (1992) has written of the importance of the maternal object meeting her infant with experiences of 'novelty, surprise, enjoyment and delight' (p. 63), which she writes 'call[s] him into being' (p. 68). Building on this idea we might say that *in the countertransference, the analyst's experience of pleasure provides a conduit for the reception of a message sent by the patient, addressed to the object, and that the mode of reception is all important* (Reis, 2009).

For Rousillon (2011a), this message originates from the drives, which seek not only discharge but also reception by the object. Here the notion of binding is correctly tied by Rousillon to the context of object relation. For Rousillon, the drive becomes a messenger that in the context of the transference 'enacts' its message. He writes,

> We can no longer think about the drives and what becomes of them without taking into account the way in which they are received, taken on board, or rejected by the object towards which they are directed; we can no longer think of drives as simply requiring to be discharged – the subjective message that they carry and convey must also be taken into consideration.
>
> (p. 32)

It would have been a technical mistake to react strongly to the tantalization created in me early in the treatment. That was the enacting of compulsive repetition that Freud wrote about as carrying a yield of pleasure for the individual, but not resulting in satisfaction. It is repetition in the service of wish gratification or as displacement. However, once the impulse to repeat was allowed to expand in almost complete freedom within the unconscious dimensions of the transference-countertransference, once it was given the right to assert itself in a definite field, as Freud wrote, a different kind of repetition was possible, one that could transmit its subjective message. Perhaps it was a shift in that unconscious field that also allowed the analyst a different sort of freedom as well – to feel less anxiety and constraint regarding the patient's tantalizing tales. At this point, Sylvie could shift from using her analyst as an object of repetition to an object of play.

In discussing the analytic treatment of repetition compulsion, Roussillon (2011b) described the potential of play to transform the constraint and inflexibility that are its hallmarks. He wrote, 'It is when play disappears that pathology begins, that the compulsion to repeat "in the same way" tends to dominate mental functioning and interpretation becomes inflexible' (p. 90). He advocates for the creation of freedom within the space of the treatment that will allow the creation of new experience by allowing the patient to once again take up what was 'given' in the initial experience. The experience of playing, he wrote, 'Thus enables a new registering of the subjective experience; it forms a new kind of subjective experience, that of the transformation of the initial subjective experience' (p. 104).

How Sylvie found an area of delight for me is a mystery. Perhaps she'd conducted an unconscious scanning (Fonagy, 2005; Sandler, 1976) of her analyst's inner world so as to determine just where to land this address. Likely it was reflective of a psychic organization Zimmer (2010) has described in which the analysand creatively appropriates and controls aspects of the analyst's affective life so as to facilitate expression of their own inner experience. Its result was for her to find meaning in the transference derived from a shared pleasure. The finding of that pleasure with me, inside the analytical experience, was an exchange where both partners contributed to the formulation of Freud's 'definite field' in a mixture (cocktail) of unconscious resonances. What seemed unique to this repetition was that the pleasure was shared. Sylvie, whose life had been dominated by a lack of feeling alive, took up with me what was 'given' in the initial experience and created a new kind of subjective experience, one that enlivened us both.

In discussing the work of Winnicott, Goldman (2017, p. 8) noted his concern for the fact that people try the best they can to communicate and unconsciously seek to find an environment which can safely be used for self-expression. Perhaps in a Winnicottian sense, Sylvie found in me an object to be created, her mother's aliveness to be reawakened and reencountered. It happened to be cocktails, but it could have been any of a number of things on the short list of what delights me. In a paradoxical way, that the discussion took this form was both irrelevant and apposite. Indeed, it might be said that the words of the conversation were not in themselves the most important aspect; their symbolic quality was not primarily involved in the work of figuration or retranscribing a forgotten or unrepresented past, but, instead, the servants of a nascent intersubjective developmental process under the sway of an instinct Freud identified as 'push[ing one] forward toward progress and the production of new forms'. Winnicott (1971b) wrote of treatment as taking place in the context of two people playing together. When the patient is unable to play, or as in this case that their play is hindered through being yoked to compulsive repetition, the analyst's efforts are meant to bring the patient to a place wherein they are able to play freely and creatively. When this can be accomplished, it results in patient and analyst 'living an experience together' (Winnicott, 1945, p. 152).

Pleasure and the object

As a developmental experience, Rousillon (2013) observed that the object's affective presence during infancy is crucial to the infant's ability to establish the feeling of satisfaction.

> The kind of affective presence shown by the object and the pleasure it takes are necessary for the experience of primary satisfaction to be set up because the infant experiences them as a reflection of his or her own satisfaction, which, as a result, becomes an acceptable experience. When the object shows no sign of satisfaction, the infant remains unaware of his or her own pleasure and satisfaction. This implies that some people have no knowledge at all of satisfaction, even though they may experience some kinds of pleasure: the affect of satisfaction, which cannot be mentally set up, remains unconscious.
> (pp. 266–267)

Such was the case for Sylvie, whose relation to early objects did not show the consistent affective presence necessary to establish her own satisfaction. This being the case lent importance to the analyst's countertransferential expression rather than his focusing on making meaning with the patient or interpreting this clinical event at the time of its occurrence.

Goldman (2017, p. 122) recently observed, 'playing' was . . . 'shorthand for Winnicott's view of therapy as a proto-symbolic, performative activity rather than one trafficking in information exchange and insight'. In this treatment, *the experience of playing* took precedence over playing as a substitutive symbolic representation for what had been absent (Ogden, 2007). For my part, offering myself as 'live company' (Alvarez, 1992) met the communication present in the patient's repetition. As a technical choice, sharing this experience with the patient rather than a painstaking reconstruction of an early reality, be it material or psychic, resulted in what Loewald (1971) has said psychoanalysis should be – a creative repetition.

Note

1 It may be important to note, as Goldman (2012) has, that for Winnicott, the intermediate area was one that exists between the polarities of activity and passivity; it is for him 'crucial as a resting *place* from the perpetual strain of keeping inner and outer separate but interrelated' (pp. 10–11) and depends on something other than Freud's demand that the patient comply with the restrictions of analysis.

References

Alvarez, A. (1992). *Live Company: Psychoanalytic Psychotherapy with Autistic, Borderline, Deprived and Abused Children*. London: Routledge.

Alvarez, A. (2012). *The Thinking Heart: Three Levels of Psychoanalytic Therapy with Disturbed Children*. London: Routledge.

Aulagnier, P. (1986). 'Naissance d'un corps, origine d'une histoire.' In: *Corps et Histoire*. Paris: Les Belles Lettres.

Balint, M. (1968). *The Basic Fault*. London: Tavistock Publications.

Bohleber, W., Fonagy, P., Jiménez, J.P., Scarfone, D., Varvin, S. & Zysman, S. (2013). 'Towards a Better Use of Psychoanalytic Concepts: A Model Illustrating Using the Concept of Enactment.' *International Journal of Psychoanalysis*, 94(3): 501–530.

Bollas, C. (2011). 'Character and Interformality.' In: A. Jemsted (Ed.) *The Christopher Bollas Reader*. New York: Routledge, pp. 238–248.

Boston Change Process Study Group. (2010). *Change in Psychotherapy: A Unifying Paradigm*. New York: Norton & Co.

Breuer, J. & Freud, S. (1893). On the Psychical Mechanism of Hysterical Phenomena. *The Standard Edition of the Complete Psychological Works of Sigmund Freud, Volume II (1893-1895): Studies on Hysteria*, pp. 1–17.

Carpy, D. (1989). 'Tolerating the Countertransference: A Mutative Process.' *International Journal of Psychoanalysis*, 70: 287–294.

Caruth, C. (2013). 'Parting Words: Trauma, Silence and Survival.' In: *Literature in the Ashes of History*. Baltimore, MD: Johns Hopkins University Press, pp. 3–17.

Cooney, A.S. (2018). 'Vitalizing Enactment: A Relational Exploration.' *Psychoanalytic Dialogues*, 28: 340–354.

Cooper, S.A. (2015). 'Reflections on the Analyst's "Good Enough" Capacity to Bear Disappointment, with Special Attention to Repetition.' *Journal of the American Psychoanalytic Association*, 63(6): 1193–1213.

Dickinson, E. (2000). *The Selected Poems of Emily Dickinson*. New York: Random House.

Fonagy, P. (2005). 'An Overview of Joseph Sandler's Key Contributions to Theoretical and Clinical Psychoanalysis.' *Psychoanalytic Inquiry*, 25(2): 120–147.

Freud, S. (1905). 'Jokes and Their Relation to the Unconscious.' In: J. Strachey (Ed. and Trans.) *The Standard Edition of the Complete Psychological Works of Sigmund Freud*, Vol. 8. London: Hogarth Press, pp. 1–238.

Freud, S. (1914). 'Remembering, Repeating and Working Through.' In: J. Strachey (Ed. and Trans.) *The Standard Edition of the Complete Psychological Works of Sigmund Freud*, Vol. 12, London: Hogarth Press, pp. 145–156.

Freud, S. (1920). 'Beyond the Pleasure Principle.' In: J. Strachey (Ed. and Trans.) *The Standard Edition of the Complete Psychological Works of Sigmund Freud*, Vol. 18. London: Hogarth Press, pp. 1–64.

Goldman, D. (2012). 'Weaving with the World: Winnicott's Re-Imagining of Reality.' *Psychoanalytic Quarterly*, 81(1): 1–23.

Goldman, D. (2017). *A Beholder's Share*. New York: Routledge.

Green, A. (2000). 'Experience and Thinking in Psychoanalytic Practice' In: *Andre Green at the Squiggle Foundation*. London: Karnac Books, pp. 1–15.

Green, A. (2005). *Key Ideas for Contemporary Psychoanalysis: Misrecognition and Recognition of the Unconscious*. New York: Brunner-Routledge.

Green, A. (2011). *Illusions and Disillusions of Psychoanalytic Work*, A. Weiler (Trans.). London: Karnac Books.

Heisterkamp, G. (2001). '"Is Psychoanalysis a Cheerless (Freud-Less) Profession?" Toward a Psychoanalysis of Joy.' *Psychoanalytic Quarterly*, 70(4): 839–870.

Lear, J. (2005). *Freud* (2nd ed.). New York: Routledge.

Loewald, H. (1965). 'Some Considerations on Repetition and Repetition Compulsion.' In: J. Lear (Ed.) *The Essential Loewald: Collected Papers and Monographs*. Hagerstown, MD: University Publishing Group, 2000, pp. 87–101.

Loewald, H. (1971). 'Some Considerations on Repetition and Repetition Compulsion.' *International Journal of Psychoanalysis*, 52: 59–66.

Ogden, T.H. (2007). 'On Talking-as-Dreaming.' *International Journal of Psychoanalysis*, 88: 575–589.

Parsons, M. (2014). *Living Psychoanalysis: From Theory to Experience*. New York: Routledge.

Peltz, R. (2012). 'Ways of Hearing: Getting Inside Psychoanalysis.' *Psychoanalytic Dialogues*, 22(3): 279–290.

Peltz, R. (2018). 'Discussion of "Vitalizing Enactment".' *Psychoanalytic Dialogues*, 28: 361–370.

Reis, B. (2009). 'Performative and Enactive Features of Psychoanalytic Witnessing: The Transference as the Scene of Address.' *International Journal of Psychoanalysis*, 90(6): 1359–1372.

Reis, B. (2010). 'Enactive Fields: An Approach to Interaction in the Kleinian-Bionian Model: Commentary on Paper by Lawrence J. Brown.' *Psychoanalytic Dialogues*, 20: 695–703.

Rosenfeld, H. (1987). *Impasse and Interpretation: Therapeutic and Anti-Therapeutic Factors in the Psychoanalytic Treatment of Psychotic, Borderline, and Neurotic Patients*. London: Routledge.

Roussillon, R. (2011a). 'Drive and Intersubjectivity.' In: *Primitive Agony and Symbolization*. London: Karnac Books, pp. 29–48.

Roussillon, R. (2011b). 'Play and Potential.' In: *Primitive Agony and Symbolization*. London: Karnac Books, pp. 89–106.
Roussillon, R. (2013). 'The Function of the Object in the Binding and Unbinding of the Drives.' *International Journal of Psychoanalysis*, 94: 257–276.
Sandler, J. (1976). 'Countertransference and Role Responsiveness.' *International Review of Psycho-Analysis*, 3: 43–47.
Scarfone, D. (2011). 'Repetition: Between Presence and Meaning.' *Canadian Journal of Psychoanalysis*, 19: 70–86.
Schafer, R. (2003). *Bad Feelings*. New York: Other Press.
Shulman, M. (2016). '"Unavoidable Satisfactions": The Analyst's Pleasure.' *Journal of the American Psychoanalytic Association*, 64(4): 697–727.
Steiner, J. (2006). 'Interpretative Enactments and the Analytic Setting.' *International Journal of Psychoanalysis*, 87(2): 315–320.
Stern, D.B. (2004). 'The Eye Sees Itself: Dissociation, Enactment, and the Achievement of Conflict.' *Contemporary Psychoanalysis*, 40: 197–237.
Winnicott, D.W. (1945). 'Primitive Emotional Development.' In: D.W. Winnicott (Ed.) *Through Paediatrics to Psycho-Analysis*. New York: Basic Books, 1958, pp. 145–156.
Winnicott, D.W. (1974). 'Fear of Breakdown.' *International Review of Psycho-Analysis*, 1: 103–107.
Winnicott, D.W. (1971a). *Playing and Reality*. London: Tavistock Publications.
Winnicott, D.W. (1971b). 'The Use of an Object and Relating Through Identifications.' In: *Playing and Reality*. New York: Routledge, pp. 86–94.
Zimmer, R.B. (2010). 'Three Psychic Organizations and Their Relation to Certain Aspects of the Creative Process.' *Psychoanalytic Quarterly*, 79(3): 629–663.

Index

action: listening by analyst 82; magical, of words 84; memory is 15, 64; in memory phenomena 59–60, 64; opposing, of primal instincts 37; performative 62–63; of repetition 60, 64; speech act theory 62–63, 68; therapeutic 50, 57; of withdrawal 74
affect-representations 90–91
Alvarez, A. 109–111
American Psychoanalytic Association 73
analyst: being-at-one with patient 54; emphasis on 82–83, 84; introjection of patient's objects 55n1; issues of boredom and confusion during session 94–95; place of listening 84; relation of form and content 80–82; silence of 75–77; understanding the patient 49–51; witnessing function of 60–61, 69
analytic mind use 49–50
anti-communication 96
anti-life force 35
Arrival (film) 21
as-if personality, identifying 34–35, 39, 44
Austin, J. L. 62

Bach, S. 65, 68
Balint, Michael 75, 76, 110
Baudrillard, J. 39, 45
Being a Character (Bollas) 13
being-at-one with 54, 90, 93, 97n2
benzodiazepines 93
'Beyond the Pleasure Principle' (Freud) 37, 102
Bion, W. R. 1–2, 10, 12,14, 17, 23–26, 28, 37, 40, 52, 54, 88–92, 97n2, 109, 111
Bollas, Christopher 7, 11, 13–14, 27–29, 35, 64, 80–82, 111
Boston Change Process Study Group 110

Botella, C. and S. 25–26, 28, 91–93
Breuer, J. 57, 59, 102
Bromberg, P. M. 38, 58–59, 62
Brown, Larry 22, 23, 50, 89, 95

Canova, Antonio 1
case vignettes: Donald and symbiont life 47–52, 54; Ines 93–97; Julie and witnessing 65–67, 68; Sylvie illustration of repetition 105–109; of zombie states 40–44
Chalmers, D. 39
chimera 3; creation of 7; by de M'Uzan 3, 7–10; essay on agony of 17; Greek mythology 7; traumatic links between analyst and patient 15–17
Clerc, Dominique 82–85, 85n1
Cocteau, Jean 1
complete normality 34
co-narration 57–58
Cooper, Steven 94, 111
countertransference 41–42, 49, 53, 111; aliveness and deadness 33–34; analyst's 54, 59, 66, 67, 101; dreaming 27, 29; failure of 109; *see also* transference; transference-countertransference
creative repetition 114; *see also* repetition
creative transformation 101

Davoine, F. 16
death drive 34, 39, 43
death instinct: concept of 37; existence of 44; idea of 33–34; patient's 41, 45n2; relation of life and 37–38, 45
demons 2, 77, 88–89, 96; as Duende 89, 96
de M'Uzan, M. 7–17, 17n1, 28, 51–52
depersonalization 8, 13–14, 34, 38

Deutsch, H. 34–36
Diamond, Michael 49–50
dreaming 2, 11, 35, 104; day- 23; facts of lived experience 23–25; first variation 23–25; Freudian beginning in 21–23; hallucination and 23; night-time 24; psychic functioning characteristic of 93; second variation 25–26; third variation 27–28; wild things of 28–30
dreams 2, 4; crazy 88; de M'Uzan's chimera in 10, 17; hallucinations or 23, 92; monsters and 2, 7, 17, 84; patient and analyst within dream space 11
'Dreams and Telepathy' (Freud) 23
duende 87; concept of 87–88

ego 8, 12, 14, 43, 59, 102: attitude of analyst's 26; boundaries 52, 97n2; development of 25; growth 53, 101; mastery of 103–105, 107; superego 38
Einfall 27
enactive, term 57, 60
enactive memory phenomena 15, 59–60, 69
enactive witnessing: concept of 57–58; experience of 67–69; memory in 59; *see also* witnessing
enactment 104, 107; conception of 109–111; mutual 58; subject of enactive witnessing 57; unconscious 51
epistemologies 17
experiences: dreaming and meaning of 23–25; of enactive witnessing 67–69; fanciful 16–17; play of children 103; pleasure and the object 113–114; process of remembering 91, 92; with reverie with patient 54; self- 51, 55n1, 60; symbolization of 79–80, 81, 84–85

Falcão, Luciane 26
False Self 43
Felman, S. 63
Ferro, A. 25
Fliess, W. 50–51, 97n1, 102
floating individuation, zone of 12, 13
form and content: analysis of relation between 80–82; magical action of words 84–85
Frankenstein (Shelley) 7
Franklin, Aretha 29
Freaky Friday (film) 51
Freud, Sigmund 1, 4, 7, 11, 12, 14, 21–23, 25–27, 29–30, 33, 37–39, 45n1, 57–60, 64, 79, 82–83, 91–93, 97n1, 101–105, 112–113, 114n1

Gabbard, G. O. 77
Garcia Lorac, Federico 87, 96; Duende in words of 87–89, 96
Gaudilliere, J. M. 16
Goldman, D. 113, 114n1
Grand, S. 61–62
Green, Andre 10, 25–26, 35, 82, 90–91
Greenberg, Jay 34, 63
Grossmark, Robert 57–58
Grotstein, J. S. 2, 23, 28, 96, 97n2

hallucinations 16; of analyst 7, 25; dreams or 2, 3, 14, 21, 23, 30; notion of 26; wild things in dreams 28–30

id 23, 53
identification 35, 39, 96; melancholic 96; patient forming, with analyst 49–51, 55n1; projective 10, 12, 15, 51–52, 89
identity 4, 7, 17; analyst's sense of 14, 51–52; boundary of, between analyst and patient 8; new approaches to 11–13; notion of 39; personal sense of 11; *Interpretation of Dreams, The* (Freud) 22
Ithier, B. 7, 10, 14–17

Jones, Grace 53

Klein, Melanie 12, 15, 45n1, 51, 64, 89

Langer, Suzanne 81
Laub, D. 59, 68
Lear, J. 102
libido 12, 38, 45n2
life instincts 33, 34, 37, 45
listening 63; analyst to patient 8, 22, 27, 29, 41, 106; deep associative 27, 77; emphasis on 82–83, 84; silence of analyst 75–77
Little, Suzanne 74
live company 114
Loewald, H. W. 57, 59–60, 63–64, 114

McDougall, Joyce 35, 96
madness 2, 3, 11, 16, 17, 55n1, 65–66, 84, 88, 96
magical realism 3
Mallarme, S. 17
marijuana 93, 94
masturbation 66–67, 108
Mead, G. H. 81
Meltzer, D. 50
Melville, Herman 9

memory: approach to 97n1; centrality of action in phenomena 59–60, 64; enactive witnessing 59; process of remembering 91, 92, 97n1; reality of 92; traumatic 63–64
Merleau-Ponty, C. 4, 17
missing persons, non-human states 34–36
monsters 2, 4, 7–10, 14, 17, 84

Nancy, Jean-Luc 4, 17, 77
narcissistic 10, 13, 23, 44, 74; cathexis 17n1, 51; libido 12; retreats 74; tendencies 51
narrative freedom 58
Nettleton, S. 80, 82
non-human states: aliveness and deadness 33–34, 36–37; missing persons 34–36; in psychotic conditions 36
normopath/normopathic 35, 44
normotic 34–35, 39, 44

object(s): analyst's introjection of patient's 55n1; identity 11; pleasure and 113–114; psychoanalytic concept of 2; symbol representing 81
Ogden, Thomas 10–14, 17, 23–24, 28, 36, 38, 40, 51–52, 54, 62, 76, 91–92, 95
'On Beginning the Treatment' (Freud) 22
ontologies 17
Orange, D. 60, 62

Parsons, Michael 54, 76–77, 104–105
Paterson, Don ix, 3
Peltz, R. 109–110
phenomena of life 37–38
philosophical zombie 39
pink Cadillacs, Franklin's metaphor 29
Plato 52
poetry, psychoanalysis and 87–88
process of remembering 91, 92
Project for a Scientific Psychology (Freud) 59–60
projective identification 10, 12, 15, 51–52, 89
Psyche and Eros 1, 4
psychic deadness 33, 37
psychoanalysis 2; act of analytic listening 84; creation of meaning 90; as creative repetition 104, 114; epistemic and ontological commitments of analyst 17; experiential aspect of treatment 3–4; magical action of words 84–85; memory and repetition 57; of patient's speech 82–84; poetry and 87–88; process of for and why 89; representation of unrepresented states 88, 88–89; silence in 73–76; symbolization of experience 79–80
'Psycho-Analysis' (Freud) 22–23

quiet, practice of psychanalysis 73–77
quieting 75

'Recommendations to Physicians' (Freud) 21, 22
regredience 26, 92–93
relationships: between form and content 81; human 42, 87, 90, 95, 107; life and death instincts 37–39, 45; memory and repetition 57, 60; patient and analyst 73–74, 76, 91; symbiont life 47–54
remembering 57, 60; act of 101; process of 91, 92, 97; repeating and 64, 101; work of 97n1
repetition: clinical illustration of 105–109; compulsion 102, 103, 104–105, 112; dark side of 102; playground and 104–105; pleasure and the object 113–114; pleasure in 101, 104–105, 112; traumatic 102–103, 105; varieties of 101–104
representations 9, 17, 17n1, 57, 88; affect 90–91; dreaming 24–26; enactive 58–59; failure of 58; form and content 80, 82; patient's 11, 51; symbolic 24, 49–50, 61, 80, 90, 92, 110, 114
reverie 7; concept of 10; dream thoughts or 24; experience with patient 54; paradoxical nature of 77; quiet analyst and 75
Rosenfeld, H. 12, 52,
Rousillion, R. 111–113
Rubens, Peter Paul 52

Salberg, J. 73
schizophrenic individuals 12, 36
Schneider, J. A. 23
Searles, Harold 3, 12, 36, 52, 77
seduction 10, 102, 107
seductive/seductiveness 43, 106
seething cauldron 23
Segal, H. 38
seizure 14, 15, 84
self-experience 51, 55n1 60
Sendak, Maurice 28
sexual masochism 108
shared madness 3
Shelley, Mary 7

silence 3; of analyst and patient 73–76; emphasis on listening 82–83, 84
Smith, Tracy K. 87–89
social link, analyst and patient 16
speech: emphasis on listening 82–83, 84; magical action of words 84–85; notion of 68–69; psychoanalysis of patient's 82–84; speech act theory 62–63
Spezzano, C. 50
Stein, Ruth 90–92
Stern, D. B. 58
Studies on Hysteria (Breuer and Freud) 57, 63
symbiont relations: analytic treatment 50; case of patient Donald 47–54; therapeutic symbiosis 12, 52, 54
symbol(s): representing experience 79–80, 81, 84–85; representing objects 81
symbolization: failures of 94; psychoanalysis of experience 79–80, 84–85; witnessing and 62
Symington, N. 43

therapeutic symbiosis 12, 52, 54
thing presentations 79
thinking: apparatus for 89; practising psychoanalysts 89–90
Thoreau, Henry David 21, 30
transference 9, 11, 76; acting as scene of address 63–64; counter- 11; maternal erotic 29; as playground 104–106; repetitions 64, 104, 107; as shared pleasure 112; theory of 102
transference-countertransference 16, 40–41, 51, 57–58, 62, 64, 91, 96, 105, 111
traumatic experience: blocked out 24; living out 57, 59, 79; narration of 61; repetition of 67–68; symbolization of 62
traumatic neurosis 102–103
True Self 43

unconscious: experience 23, 29, 80, 82, 95; fantasy/phantasy 3, 10, 24, 40, 42, 51, 59; Freud's writing on 21–23, 27; minds 8, 14–15; processes 4, 14, 22, 29, 54, 92; psychic spaces 13–14; relation 2, 4, 50; thought 22, 105
'Unconscious, The' (Freud) 22
unconscious communication 7, 16, 17; conceptualization of 28; patient's 11, 27–28; role in enactment 58

vinculo 3, 77

war neurosis 102
wild things, dreaming and hallucinating 28–30
Winnicott, D. W. 2, 4, 12, 17n1, 24–25, 34, 43, 49–50, 53, 68, 74–76, 84, 88, 104–105, 107, 110, 113, 114n1
witnessing: case vignette (Julie) 65–67, 68; concept of 57; expanding notion of 62; experience of enactive 67–69; function of analyst 60–61, 69; memories in feelings 64; symbolization and 62; testimony of 63; traumatic repetition 63–64, 68–69
word presentations 79
'Work of the Negative, The' (Green) 25
Wright, C. D. 79, 82, 84
WWI 102

zero point 43
zombie states 33, 39; analytic engagement 40; forms of aliveness and deadness 33, 36–37; missing persons 34–36; non-human states in characterological disorders 34–36; non-human states in psychotic conditions 36; psychic deadness 33–34; relation of life and death instincts 33, 37–39; vignette 40–44
zone of floating individuation 12, 13